Know-It-All

Classical
Music

Know-It-All

Classical Music

The 50 Most Significant Genres, Composers & Forms, Each Explained in Under a Minute >

Editor **Dr. Joanne Cormac**
Foreword **David Pickard**

Contributors

Robert Adlington
Edward Breen
Dr. Joanne Cormac
George Hall
Katy Hamilton
Kenneth Hamilton
Monika Hennemann
Elizabeth Kelly
Emily MacGregor
Simon Paterson
Owen Rees
Hugo Shirley
Alexandra Wilson

—WELLFLEET—
P R E S S

Quarto is the authority on a wide range of topics.

Quarto educates, entertains and enriches the lives of
our readers—enthusiasts and lovers of hands-on living.

www.quartoknows.com

First published in the United States of America
in 2017 by Wellfleet Press, a member of
Quarto Publishing Group USA Inc.
142 West 36th Street, 4th Floor
New York, New York 10018
www.QuartoKnows.com

10 9 8 7 6 5 4 3 2 1

ISBN: 978-1-57715-150-0

This book was conceived, designed,
and produced by

Ivy Press
An imprint of The Quarto Group
The Old Brewery, 6 Blundell Street
London N7 9BH, United Kingdom
T (0)20 7700 6700 F (0)20 7700 8066

Publisher Susan Kelly
Creative Director Michael Whitehead
Editorial Director Tom Kitch
Commissioning Editor Stephanie Evans
Project Editor Fleur Jones
Designer Ginny Zeal
Illustrator Nicky Ackland-Snow
Picture Researcher Katie Greenwood

Printed in China

CONTENTS

FOREWORD
David Pickard

In November 2015, I took on the role of director
of the UK's BBC Proms, a major classical music festival. When Robert
Newman and Henry Wood founded this famous festival in 1895, their aim
was to bring great classical music to the widest possible audience. They
saw their role as educational in the broadest sense. More than 120 years
later those principles remain unchanged, and my intention is to continue
and develop what Newman and Wood began and find new ways to extend
the reach of the Proms in the twenty-first century. The thousands of
people who flock to concerts each summer, and the millions more who
watch or listen to broadcasts, are testament to the power of classical
music to thrill and entertain, no matter who you are.

Recently, I sat next to a retired lady at dinner who was enthusing about the classical music appreciation classes she was attending. "We're doing Mahler next week!" she told me with relish. She had loved classical music all her life and was embracing the opportunity to explore her passion in more detail, adding another dimension to her listening. In her quest for greater knowledge about classical music she was lucky enough to have that precious commodity: time.

For those who don't yet have that luxury, I can't think of a better way to start—or continue—learning than with *Know-It-All Classical Music*. Dipping into this book feels like a visit to my favorite kind of museum—the sort that reflects a broad range of art (often personally chosen) in two or three rooms of exhibits. A museum or gallery that gives you a snapshot of its subject without leaving you feeling overwhelmed.

So, in *Know-It-All Classical Music,* I have enjoyed seeing how the writers explain "The Symphony" or "Serialism" in a handful of words—capturing the essence of a subject and giving the reader the chance to explore further should they wish. The book proves that it is possible to be brief, succinct, and insightful without being patronizing or simplistic. I found myself trying (and failing) to catch out the authors—searching for key moments in the history of classical music that must surely be overlooked in a volume as concise as this. But, miraculously, every significant development seems to be covered and the right cues are there for finding out more.

I share the widespread current concern about the downgrading of arts subjects as part of the school curriculum and believe that young people should have access to the best of classical music. However, we should remember that many adults harbor regrets about giving up a musical instrument as a child before they had fully mastered it, or not having paid attention during music classes at school. For those for whom classical music is now an important part of their lives, this book will go a long way toward enhancing their listening.

A popular choice as a first instrument to learn, the piano has evolved through many forms over its long history, from harpsichord to pianoforte to the upright and grand pianos we know today.

INTRODUCTION

Joanne Cormac

Millions of people enjoy excerpts from classical music's "greatest hits." Mendelssohn's "Wedding March" from *A Midsummer Night's Dream*, Handel's *Messiah* and the opening of Beethoven's *Symphony No. 5* are enduring in the concert hall and ubiquitous in popular culture. Some may already be incidental fans through film music, relishing the drama of, say, Wagner's "Ride of the Valkyries" in *Apocalypse Now*. For many, however, lesser-known pieces might seem impenetrable or overly long, and as a result the thought of attending a concert offers little attraction. To the "uninitiated," probing further can appear daunting or old-fogey.

The idea of being "initiated" into classical music suggests that it's not for everyone. But classical music is *everywhere* and is for *everyone*. It is available free of charge on websites such as YouTube and Spotify, while live concerts are increasingly cheap and easy to attend. So if price or availability is not the issue, what is? Classical music perhaps suffers—unfairly—from an image problem. Some see it as an art form that is incomprehensible, snooty, and foreign. This is a real shame because there's so much to be gained from both playing and listening to this music. There's the intellectual benefit, not to mention the sheer satisfaction that learning a musical instrument brings. There's the social enjoyment of playing with others, or of sharing the experience of live performance. And there's the emotional effect that listening to classical music can create. Classical music does spine-tingling, heart-breaking, uplifting, and thrilling like no other type of music.

The aim of this book is to help open up classical music to new audiences and to give existing ones fresh information to increase their enjoyment. It aims to dispel some of the myths, to explain the off-putting jargon, and to help listeners understand and appreciate the beauties of this rich and varied repertoire: There really is something for everyone.

The symphony was one of the key musical genres of the eighteenth and nineteenth centuries. Ludwig van Beethoven's nine symphonies are among the most enduringly popular.

The book is divided into sections that progress chronologically to give a sense of how classical music has developed over time—from the earliest instruments and monastic plainchant to the electronic music of the late-twentieth and twenty-first centuries (though, of course, you can dip in and out as it suits). Naturally, the story is really rather messier and more complicated than this smooth transition from era to era, composer to composer, and style to style suggests. However, by selecting the key players, forms, and genres, I hope to encourage you to take the creative journey and explore further and wider into the classical music world.

Each of the seven sections has its own glossary, which explains unfamiliar terms, and one profile of a maestro—singer, musician, or conductor—a true master of their art. The 50 topics themselves are easily assimilated in under a minute, using just 300 words and one picture. Many of the topics focus on particular composers and pinpoint particular pieces. Composers are naturally an important part of the story of classical music, but there are other parts: institutions, performers, technology, and audiences to name but a few. By spotlighting issues like patronage or historically informed performance, and developments such as recording, the book gives some sense of this broader story. Readers might notice that opera plays a very limited role in this book, as does jazz. These genres, whose stories are inevitably intertwined with that of classical music, are the focus of other volumes.

Inevitably, there are some wonderful composers, and some important genres, events, and issues that could not be included. So I urge readers not to end their classical music journey here: Keep exploring and listening to new composers. Enjoy!

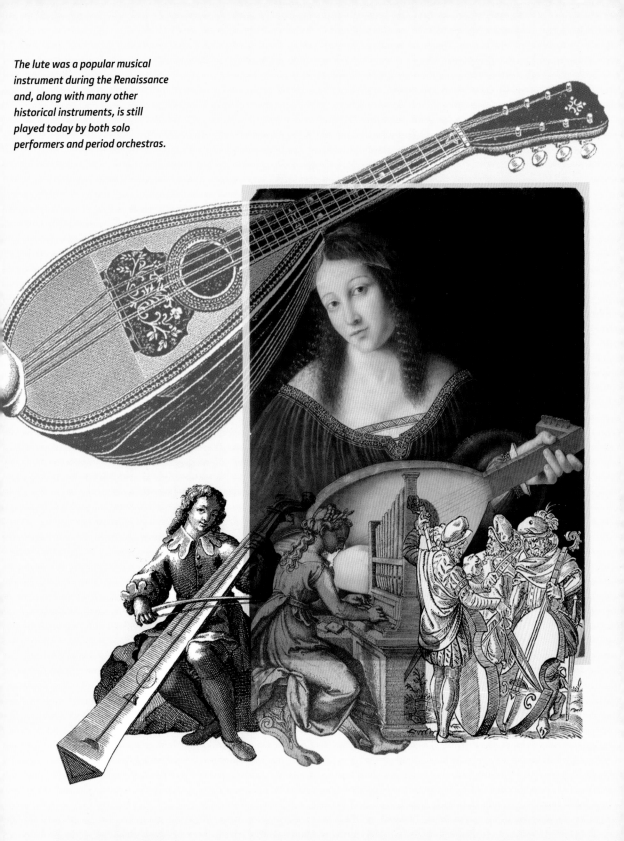

The lute was a popular musical instrument during the Renaissance and, along with many other historical instruments, is still played today by both solo performers and period orchestras.

THE MIDDLE AGES

Ars nova (Latin: "new art") Style of polyphony from fourteenth-century France. The innovations of this style focused on rhythmic flexibility, allowing for the division of note values into groups of two as well as three and for shorter note values to be used. The style coincided with a new notational system that offered greater precision in notating rhythms. Detractors of *Ars nova* advocated the older style of the late thirteenth century, known as *Ars antiqua* or ancient art. Some theorists objected to the use of duple division because triple division was deemed perfect and associated with the Trinity.

centonization Composing by using a patchwork of recurring, preexisting, melodic shapes. The concept is usually used in connection with plainchant in which certain melodic formulas regularly occur.

Council of Trent A Roman Catholic church council convened by Pope Paul III that met in northern Italy between 1545 and 1563 to discuss how to respond to the Reformation. Part of the discussion involved music, attempting to standardize the liturgy, restricting the use of music taken from secular sources, and restricting or limiting the use of polyphonic music because complicated music with several parts obscured the words of the text. However, the council did not make these ideas official policy.

Gregorian chant Unaccompanied monophonic vocal music to which parts of the liturgy were sung in Roman Catholic church services. Early eighth-century books of liturgical texts are attributed to Pope Gregory I (hence the term "Gregorian chant" to describe the central branch of plainchant sung in medieval western Europe), although there is little evidence that he was involved in composing or standardizing chant.

isorhythm (equal rhythm) A term used to describe the device of employing a recurring rhythmic segment or talea. The repeating rhythm is usually found in the slow-moving chant voice known as the tenor. The tenor may also repeat a melodic segment (a color). Such melodic and rhythmic segments gave coherent structures to long compositions.

liturgy Established forms and patterns of worship used by a faith community, most commonly associated with Judaism and Christianity. The term often refers specifically to the body of texts and rituals used in religious services.

monophony A type of musical texture involving only one unaccompanied melody.

motet The most important form of polyphonic vocal music of the Middle Ages and Renaissance. It was created in the early thirteenth century by adding new texts to the upper (highest) voices of a self-contained section of organum. The lower part tended to move slowly and was derived from plainchant with a Latin text. Other parts moved more quickly and often had unrelated Latin or (sometimes secular) French texts. From the Renaissance period motets were usually settings of Latin sacred texts and intended for Catholic church services. From the fifteenth century the motet became a choral setting of a religious text for four or more voices.

neumes (Latin: "gesture") Symbols that resemble the accents used in French, which were used in the earliest forms of musical notation. They were placed above the words to be sung to indicate the number of notes assigned to a syllable, the direction of the melody (whether it should move up or down or whether a note should be repeated), and the rhythm. Neumes could only indicate the shape of the melody, not specific pitches. They worked as reminders to singers who knew the melodies already because they had learned them by ear. Heighted neumes, at varying heights above the text to indicate the size of the interval between each note, developed in the tenth and eleventh centuries. This meant that the shape of the melody could be notated with more precision.

notation A way to write down music that was invented for church music. Over the centuries it became increasingly sophisticated, allowing composers to record their work with precision and instruct performers on how to play a piece.

organum Term for an early form of melodic harmonization in which two or more voices sing different notes in agreeable combinations. The simplest type of organum combines a melody in one voice with a drone accompaniment (a single sustained note) in another. Another common form consists of doubling a melody so that the voices move in parallel a consonant interval apart. Organum flourished from c. 900 to 1200.

upper voice When a piece of music involves more than one part sung or played at the same time, the highest of the parts is known as the upper voice.

vibrato A style of singing or playing in which the performer makes the pitch of a note waver in order to intensify the tone. The use of vibrato has gone in and out of fashion. Constant vibrato is now the norm, but nineteenth-century performers used it sparingly, and early music is usually performed without vibrato in order to comply with what we understand of the performing practices of the time.

THE BEGINNINGS

The founding father of ancient Greek music was Pythagoras. He is attributed with the discovery of musical ratios, a way of measuring distances between notes. When passing a blacksmiths' forge one day he heard different notes sounding from smiths working at their anvils. He weighed their hammers and deduced the relationship between their weight and the notes he heard. However, this charming tale has a sting: Pythagoras should have weighed the anvils and not the hammers! The Greeks thought of music intertwined with science; for them it was an orderly system enmeshed with nature. This notion of music as a system of numbers was continued in the Middle Ages by the scholar Boethius, whose *De institutione musica* (*The Fundamentals of Music*) drew heavily on Greek sources. But Greeks also thought deeply about the philosophical nature of music. Plato in his *Republic* and *Timaeus* and Aristotle in his *Politics* discuss music's nature, effects, and proper uses. Almost 50 fragments of Greek music survive, all single-line melodies, which we suspect from pictorial evidence were performed to the accompaniment of plucked instruments, the lyre or kithara.

RELATED TOPICS

See also
PLAINCHANT
page 18

3-SECOND BIOGRAPHIES
BOETHIUS
c. 480–c. 524
Roman scholar and influential early medieval philosopher

ISIDORE OF SEVILLE
c. 560–636
Scholar born into a family of saints in Spain who served as Archbishop of Seville

EXPERT
Edward Breen

3-SECOND NOTE
Although we can trace music-making to the Stone Age, historians consider ancient Greece the earliest civilization to have left substantial evidence of a musical culture.

3-MINUTE REFRAIN
In the seventh century, Isidore of Seville bemoaned, "Unless sounds are remembered by men, they perish, for they cannot be written down." Interestingly, he seems not to have known about ancient Greek music notations; for him there simply wasn't a technology for notating music, there was just an oral tradition. This opens fascinating questions about history and the role of music: when music notation was (re)developed c. 900 it recorded an existing musical tradition, a story that was already well underway.

The Pythagorean vision of orderly systems was not unique to music; he believed order applied to the whole universe.

PLAINCHANT

Plainchant refers to the many different types of chant used at various times throughout the history of the Roman Catholic church, and it presents modern musicians with an intriguing list of unanswered questions. At first it was an oral tradition, performed long before music notation. Around 800, when Charles I (Charlemagne) sought to unify church services throughout his kingdom, it was written in a form of notes that are merely an aide-mémoire for the shape of the melody and show neither exactly how high or low to sing, nor how long each note should be. The earliest chant notation comprises such contour lines (neumes) drawn above words called unheighted neumes. As music notation developed, neumes were eventually written against a ruled ladder (staff) to indicate the distances between notes. Since plainchant is made of just one part, a single melody (monophony), it tends to be performed simply and slowly by a solo singer, or a group of people all singing the same note together (unison). Plainchant is not simple music though: it ranges from repetitive and mesmeric formulas to complex and ornate melodies.

3-SECOND NOTE

Plainchant is timeless: it was sung long before music notation existed and is today one of the most recognizable sounds of medieval and monastic life.

3-MINUTE REFRAIN

To a medieval singer, plainchant was as much music as it was prayer, and this preserves its regular use in church services (liturgy) right up to the present day. Now, it is the sound most readily associated with the Middle Ages, and due to its simple texture and calm pace many listeners find it relaxing and meditative. In 1994, a CD of chant performed by the monks of Santo Domingo de Silos sold around six million copies worldwide.

RELATED TOPICS
See also
POLYPHONY
page 24

MASS SETTINGS
page 34

3-SECOND BIOGRAPHIES
ST GREGORY (THE GREAT)
c. 540–604
Pope Gregory I
(Latin: Gregorius I)

CHARLEMAGNE
c. 742–814
The King of the Franks, also known as Charles the Great or Charles I (Latin: Carolus Magnus)

EXPERT
Edward Breen

One family of plainchant is known as Gregorian chant, named after St. Gregory. Legend has it that these chants were dictated directly by the Holy Spirit, symbolized as a dove that sang into the saint's ear.

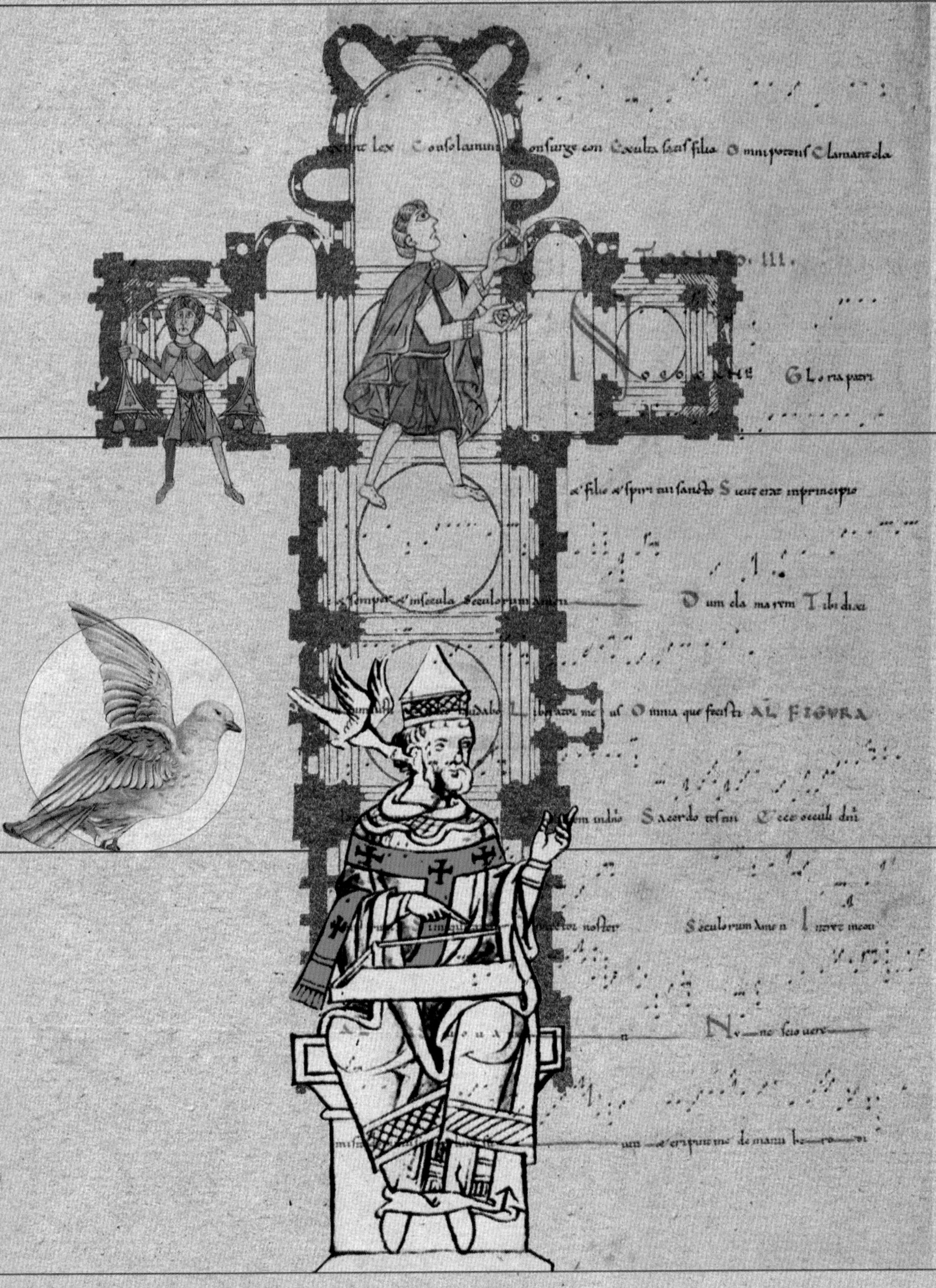

HILDEGARD OF BINGEN

Famous for her prophecies

throughout and beyond her native Germany, Hildegard of Bingen (1098–1179) corresponded with popes, kings, and Queen Eleanor of Aquitaine on diplomatic and intellectual matters. One account of her visions, *Scivias* ("know the ways of the Lord") contains an illustration of her working alongside the monk Volmar, as a vision descends like rays from above. This has intriguing similarities to both the biblical story of the Apostles (Pentecost) and of St. Gregory receiving plainchant. Hildegard wrote around 72 songs (some liturgical) and a morality play called *Ordo virtutum* (*The Order of the Virtues*). Similar to plainchant but distinct from it, Hildegard's music is also monophonic albeit more adventurous, if not audaciously so. Her melodies can exceed two octaves yet, despite such high and low extremes, her music is crafted from small numbers of repeating elemental patterns (a process called centonization). Her lyrics are also profound; they share the apocalyptic language of her visions and draw on brilliant and dramatic imagery. She is the first medieval figure known to have overseen the compilation and copying of her own works. Sadly, the manuscript of *Scivias* has been missing since the Second World War.

3-SECOND NOTE
Abbess, writer, and composer, Hildegard of Bingen established her own convent, received visions, and wrote scientific works, and her life offers us great insight into the twelfth century.

3-MINUTE REFRAIN
Hildegard believed her visions came directly from God, but writing in his 1985 book, *The Man Who Mistook His Wife for a Hat*, neurologist Dr. Oliver Sacks noted the similarity of Hildegard's visions to experiences of severe migraine sufferers. In her two surviving *Codices*, Hildegard's illustrations of her visions show brightly colored figures radiating from a central point with prominent points of light, all consistent with current medical understanding of migraines.

RELATED TOPICS
See also
PLAINCHANT
page 18

EMMA KIRKBY
page 22

3-SECOND BIOGRAPHIES
ELEANOR OF AQUITAINE
c. 1122–1204
One of the most powerful women in western Europe, eventually Queen consort of France and of England; patron of many literary figures including the Bernart de Ventadorn

VOLMAR
d. 1173
Monk who is most likely to have taught Hildegard music notation. Their friendship embodies a kind of love cultivated by religious men and women of the twelfth century

EXPERT
Edward Breen

Born into a noble family, Hildegard's parents promised her to the Church when she was eight. She spent much of her young life confined to a stone cell.

1949
Born in Camberley, Surrey

1974
Makes her first appearance with the Consort of Musicke

1975
Records for the first time with the Academy of Ancient Music (AAM)

1979
Her recording of Handel's *Messiah* with the AAM under Hogwood is released

1983
Makes her stage debut in Bruges in Locke and Christopher Gibbons' *Cupid and Death*

1989
Sings in three early eighteenth-century settings of *The Judgement of Paris* at the BBC Proms, and makes her US debut in Handel's *Orlando*

1999
Voted Artist of the Year by listeners to Classic FM

2007
Made a Dame Commander of the British Empire and is also listed in a survey of *BBC Music Magazine* critics as one of the 20 Greatest Sopranos

2011
Awarded the Queen's Medal for Music

EMMA KIRKBY

With her unique voice and

approach to singing, soprano Emma Kirkby has become not just one of the best-loved vocalists of our time but also one of the most influential.

When she launched her career at the beginning of the 1970s, the early-music movement was just starting to move beyond its specialist niche and to connect with a wider public. Performers, promoters, and record companies were to discover—perhaps to their surprise—that there was a new and largely untapped audience for music from the Baroque and Renaissance periods, and even earlier; in catering for it, they would soon expand beyond such familiar names as Bach and Handel into realms hitherto known only to scholars.

Kirkby would quickly become one of the most instantly recognizable performers of this new-old repertoire, a favorite not only with specialist musicians who led period-instrument ensembles and orchestras, but also—through burgeoning recordings—with a wider public. Relationships with groups such as Anthony Rooley's Consort of Musicke and Christopher Hogwood's Academy of Ancient Music would be long-lasting and extremely productive; others would follow with the Freiburger Barockorchester, the Orchestra of the Age of Enlightenment and Florilegium.

Kirkby has always possessed a number of advantages over her singing rivals. One is her musicianship, allowing her to acquire a substantial repertoire and to perform it flawlessly in tune.

Another is her voice itself, a distinctively lucid instrument quite different in character and color from those usually associated with music from the Romantic period or later: whereas the previous standard soprano model was large and occasionally unwieldy, Kirkby's instrument is small, but also pure, exact, and true. Without the vibrato of the operatic diva, she avoids an overbearing tone or any suggestion of wobble. Though we can't know with any certainty how "early music" sounded, Emma Kirkby's pure voice is often recognized as the quintessential sound of early-music performance.

Additionally, her sensitivity to words—and especially English words—has been exemplary, while her repertoire has ranged from medieval composers such as Hildegard of Bingen up to Bach, Handel, and their contemporaries and into the classical period of Haydn and Mozart. Rarely appearing on the operatic stage, she has made a uniquely successful career as an internationally acclaimed period specialist in the recording studio as well as on the concert platform.

George Hall

POLYPHONY

Polyphonic textures were

described by a music theorist in the ninth century but were likely practiced in much earlier oral traditions. However, in the twelfth century increasingly complex polyphony developed. The simplest type of polyphony (as described in the ninth century), called organum, takes a plainchant tune and embellishes it with another tune. In "parallel organum" the tunes are the same, but one is higher than the other so they form harmony as they are sung simultaneously. In "oblique organum" the notes move in opposite directions to each other, and in "free organum" notes may move in either direction. Over time this became more complex: the two tunes could move at different speeds, or many notes might embellish a single sustained note of chant (or vice-versa). The slow-moving chant voice was called the tenor, and, with some ingenious organization, two and even three other tunes could be added to the chant to create elaborate and sonorous textures. Organum gave rise to many developments, but the most fascinating is called a motet, in which passages of liturgical organum had secular and often somewhat racy texts added to one of the tunes. In the middle of all this, plainchant remained present like a golden thread.

RELATED TOPICS
See also
PLAINCHANT
page 18

TROUBADOURS & TROUVÈRES
page 26

3-SECOND BIOGRAPHIES
LEONIN & PEROTIN
fl. 1150s–c. 1201
& fl. c. 1200
Two composers famous for their organa, both musicians at the newly built Cathedral of Notre Dame, Paris

EXPERT
Edward Breen

3-SECOND NOTE
Polyphony—two or more tunes performed simultaneously—came into being in the 1200s as music-writing entered a new phase: a "technological" transformation.

3-MINUTE REFRAIN
The thirteenth century saw new systems of writing and new systems of book production, and Paris, a fashion leader, was at the helm of these developments. With its impressive acoustic, the cathedral of Notre Dame would have been a rewarding place to sing two different notes together, creating polyphonic music that resounded throughout the stone building. In this age, music becomes increasingly associated with a tangible object—the book.

Begun in 1163, the Cathedral of Notre Dame in Paris was one of the first to use flying buttresses. These supports allowed for taller, thinner walls, which contributed to the generous echo associated with large Gothic buildings.

TROUBADOURS & TROUVÈRES

3-SECOND NOTE

More than mere wandering minstrels, troubadours and trouvères were poet-musicians who exemplified aristocratic music-making through the use of stylized lyrics and highly wrought emotions.

3-MINUTE REFRAIN

A key theme in medieval lyric poetry is *Courtly Love (fin d'amours)*, a particularly rich vein in troubadour works. The essential outline is an exploration of unrequited love between the poet and a high-born unobtainable lady. Highly stylized poetry presents an idealized form of womanhood before which the poet must sublimate his own desires. This tradition was later conflated with devotion to the Virgin Mary, keenly demonstrating the ever-blurred boundaries between sacred and secular in medieval life.

The works of the troubadours

and trouvères represent two important strands of medieval monophony, but unlike plainchant these songs are largely secular and were written in the vernacular (local) language. The troubadour tradition is one of lyric poetry written in the old Occitan language from today's southern France and flourished 1100–1350, after which both they, and their Provençal culture, began to wain. Troubadours were often of high birth and their songs address concerns about social rank and frequently attempt to describe innermost emotional states. There is some evidence that troubadours wrote their poetry (lyric) and then taught it to minstrels to sing. The notation that survives is like plainsong in that it relays pitch but not rhythm. The trouvère tradition was a slightly later phenomenon written in the Old French dialect from today's northern France. It drew key influences from the troubadour tradition and was influenced and encouraged by Eleanor of Aquitaine whose son, Richard I (Lionheart), was a famous trouvère. It displays a keen interest in longer narrative poetry such as the Lai, a long song with many verses in different styles interwoven by a common narrative. Arguably, this tradition extends to the great composer Guillaume de Machaut.

RELATED TOPICS

See also
PLAINCHANT
page 18

HILDEGARD OF BINGEN
page 20

GUILLAUME DE MACHAUT
page 28

3-SECOND BIOGRAPHIES

BERNART DE VENTADORN
c. 1130/40–c. 1190/1200
The most famous troubadour

LA COMTESSA DE DIA
fl. late 12th century
Trobairitz (female troubadour) from whom we have surviving lyrics but whose true identity is shrouded in mystery

EXPERT

Edward Breen

The works of the troubadours and the trouvères share similar themes, but they also reveal political and religious differences between neighboring cultures.

GUILLAUME DE MACHAUT

3-MINUTE REFRAIN
Machaut wrote 17 motets early in his career that form a narrative: a soul's journey as it searches for union with God. His motets frequently combine a plainchant Latin tenor with French poetry in an upper voice, and Machaut frequently uses this multitextual situation to align the traditional trouvère courtly devotion to a lady with the Catholic pilgrims' devotion to the Virgin Mary.

The fourteenth century saw

significant innovations in music notation that allowed for a greater complexity and specificity of rhythm. At the time it was referred to as *Ars nova* and contrasted with the *Ars antiqua* of earlier polyphony. As heir to the great trouvère tradition, Guillaume de Machaut (1300–77) didn't just write sacred music, he also wrote many love songs, some monophonic but some for up to four voices, and this large proportion of secular music reflects a generalized decline of the church during the century. Secular music now occupied an increasing place in intellectual musical life. That said, one of Machaut's most famous compositions is his *Messe de Nostre Dame* (*Mass of Our Lady*), a setting of the texts used at each Catholic Mass service (mass ordinary). This was the first time these texts were set to music by one composer to make a coherent cycle, called a *cyclic mass*. Four of the six movements in Machaut's mass use the new *Ars nova* technique of isorhythm, in which the slow plainchant tune that runs through much medieval polyphony was repeated several times with slightly differing rhythms—a process made possible by the invention of new notation. This allowed Machaut to write longer and more complex polyphonic textures.

RELATED TOPICS
See also
PLAINCHANT
page 18

TROUBADOURS & TROUVÈRES
page 26

MASS SETTINGS
page 34

3-SECOND BIOGRAPHY
PHILIPPE DE VITRY
1291–1361
Like Machaut, a musician, poet, and churchman and, similarly, a leading figure in the French *Ars nova*

EXPERT
Edward Breen

The late flowering of a trouvère tradition in Machaut's works offers insights into the strict hierarchy of medieval courtly society and the clearly defined roles of noble men and women.

THE RENAISSANCE

THE RENAISSANCE
GLOSSARY

a cappella (Italian: "in chapel style") The instruction a cappella usually refers to choral or other types of vocal music sung without an instrumental accompaniment.

canon (Latin: "rule") A type of musical imitation in which all voices sing or play exactly the same melody, but enter after different intervals of time.

chanson (French: "song") A term commonly used with reference to polyphonic (a composition with several simultaneous, independent musical lines) songs of the medieval and Renaissance periods with French texts.

dissonance Two or more notes played together that produce a discord, which is jarring to the ear. Playing adjacent notes in the scale will produce a dissonance. Traditionally, in classical music dissonances are "resolved" with a consonant chord, which sounds harmonious, stable, and complete. However, dissonance has often been used for expressive reasons, in order to aid expression of madrigal texts. Composers in the nineteenth century experimented further with dissonance, introducing new harmonies, and avoiding or prolonging the time until resolution. In the twentieth century many composers were influenced by Schoenberg's idea of the "emancipation of the dissonance," treating traditionally dissonant chords as stable harmonies.

imitation A compositional device in which a melodic line is "imitated" in another part by repeating it exactly. Often the repeat will begin on a different pitch. Imitation is common in polyphonic music, particularly fugues and canons. It has a long history: the technique is found in organum and motets.

madrigal (Italian *madrigale*: "song in the mother tongue") Vocal composition, usually for two or three voices, that emerged in Italy at the end of the thirteenth century. The texts were usually secular (often a satirical or love poem), though madrigals on religious texts do exist. The later form is better known; madrigals became the most important secular genre of sixteenth-century Italy. They were musical settings of various types of Italian poetry, such as sonnets. Composers placed considerable emphasis on enriching the meaning of the words, exploring new expressive and dramatic effects. Sixteenth-century madrigals do not use refrains or repeated lines, which distinguishes them from the fourteenth-century madrigal. (They are only related in name.) Each line of poetry is set to new music. Most madrigals were for between four and six voices.

Mass The most important service in the Roman Catholic church. It evolved from commemorations of the last supper of Jesus and his disciples and Jesus' subsequent sacrifice for the atonement of sin. The central act involves celebrating "communion": a re-enactment of the last supper in which the priest consecrates the bread and the wine which symbolizes the body and blood of Jesus. Over time other texts, prayers, and rituals were added. Some texts for the Mass, such as readings and sermons, vary each day, whereas other parts, known as the Ordinary of the Mass, do not change, and are often set to music. The sung parts of the Mass Ordinary include the Introit (a psalm sung while the priest enters), the Kyrie (in which celebrants ask for mercy), the Gloria (praising the glory of God), the Credo (reciting the key teachings of the faith), the Offertory (a chant sung on a psalm text while the priest prepares the bread and wine), the Sanctus (the final part of the prayer of consecration of the bread and wine), and the Agnus Dei (invocations to the Lamb of God to grant mercy and peace).

requiem Roman Catholic Mass for the Dead. The liturgy follows that of the Mass Ordinary, but the Gloria and Credo are omitted and the Dies Irae (Latin: "day of wrath") is added. The Dies Irae poem was traditionally sung to a plainchant melody.

stile antico (Italian: "old style") Term used to describe historically conscious church music written after the mid-seventeenth century in the old polyphonic style associated with Palestrina. Features associated with this music include avoidance of dance rhythms, use of scoring for full choir, imitative textures, and a traditional approach to dissonance.

vibrato A style of singing or playing in which a performer makes the pitch of a note waver in order to intensify the tone. The use of vibrato has gone in and out of fashion. Constant vibrato is now the norm, but nineteenth-century performers used it sparingly, and early music is usually performed without vibrato in order to comply with what we understand of the performing practices of the time.

word painting A compositional technique in which the composer tries to reflect a text's meaning in quite a specific, decorative way. For example, if the text referred to climbing the composer might depict this in a passage of ascending notes. The technique is particularly associated with sixteenth-century madrigals, but can also be found in later Baroque music.

MASS SETTINGS

In the fifteenth century it became common for composers to set five texts from the Mass—Kyrie, Gloria, Credo, Sanctus, and Agnus Dei—as a musically unified polyphonic work. Among the earliest to write such cyclic Masses were English composers Dunstaple and Power, and from the second half of the century all of the principal European composers contributed to the genre, including Du Fay, Ockeghem, Obrecht, and Josquin. The pre-existing musical material used in each movement of a Mass was often a plainchant melody, but might also be a secular tune such as "L'homme armé" (on which dozens of Masses were based), or a single voice part from a polyphonic chanson. In the sixteenth century the most important type of Mass became the "parody" or "imitation" Mass, in which the musical material was derived from all the voices of a polyphonic piece, such as a motet, madrigal, or chanson, although use of secular models was discouraged in the period of the Counter-Reformation. Masses were frequently vehicles for technical display by composers, using devices such as canon, particularly in the Agnus Dei. Prominent Mass composers in the later Renaissance were Morales, Palestrina, Lassus, and Victoria.

RELATED TOPICS
See also
JOSQUIN DESPREZ
page 36

GIOVANNI PIERLUIGI
DA PALESTRINA
page 40

3-SECOND BIOGRAPHIES
CARLO BORROMEO
1538–84
Cardinal Archbishop of Milan who commissioned Mass settings in a simplified style designed to make the words audible to the listener

WILLIAM BYRD
1539/40–1623
Catholic English composer who published three Mass settings in the 1590s (celebrating Mass in Protestant England was illegal)

TOMÁS LUIS DE VICTORIA
c. 1548–1611
Spanish composer and chaplain to Empress María of Austria

EXPERT
Owen Rees

Singers give voice to Mass settings during religious worship to express their beliefs and traditions.

3-SECOND NOTE
The largest-scale pieces of the Renaissance, Masses were multi-movement works, unified by using the same material in each movement, and sung liturgically.

3-MINUTE REFRAIN
The Requiem is a distinct subgenre of Renaissance Mass setting. The movements set in polyphony vary, but usually include the Introit (beginning with the word "Requiem" from which the genre gets its name), Kyrie, Offertory, Sanctus, Agnus Dei, and Communion. Italian composers also usually set the Sequence "Dies iræ." The most famous Requiem of the period is Victoria's six-voice *Officium defunctorum* composed in 1603, a work of supreme poignancy and solemnity composed for the funeral rites of the Empress María of Austria.

JOSQUIN DESPREZ

3-SECOND NOTE
Josquin is revered as one of the greatest Renaissance composers, both for his consummate technique and for his reinforcing of links between music and text.

3-MINUTE REFRAIN
In recent scholarship there have arisen robust challenges to the notion of Josquin's supreme reputation during his lifetime, alongside fierce arguments concerning how many works should be included in his œuvre. No other Renaissance composer has been examined so critically in these respects, and the debates reflect the significance given to Josquin as a pivotal figure in Western music history and as the composer of some of the most mesmerizing works of the period.

Josquin, who was born in the mid-fifteenth century and died in 1521, achieved a prodigious international reputation during the sixteenth century. The first significant publisher of polyphony, Ottaviano Petrucci, favored his music above that of his contemporaries, and so strong was the appetite for Josquin's works in the decades after his death that many pieces were issued with false attributions to him. Like numerous northern-European composers of his time, he found employment and patronage in Italy, including as a singer in the Papal Choir and in the service of the great Sforza and Este families in Milan and Ferrara, but the last and longest part of his career (from 1504 until his death) was spent as Provost of the Collegiate Church of Notre Dame in Condé-sur-l'Escaut, France. The very substantial body of works ascribed to Josquin is dominated by Masses, motets, and French chansons. His output reveals the increasing importance of imitative writing, where the texture is built from overlapping statements of a motive distributed among all voices. Josquin's imaginative and ingeniously diverse crafting of large-scale structure and small-scale musical devices was frequently inspired by the texts he was setting.

RELATED TOPICS
See also
MASS SETTINGS
page 34

WORDS & MUSIC
page 38

3-SECOND BIOGRAPHIES
ERCOLE D'ESTE
1431–1505
Duke of Ferrara and Josquin's employer at the Ferrarese court, 1503–4; he was the dedicatee of Josquin's *Missa Hercules Dux Ferrariæ*, and commissioned the motet *Miserere mei Deus*

OTTAVIANO PETRUCCI
1466–1539
Italian publisher and pioneer in the printing of polyphonic music at the beginning of the sixteenth century; gave pride of place to Josquin's works

EXPERT
Owen Rees

Martin Luther (1483–1546) declared Josquin master of the notes: "they must do as he wishes . . . other masters of singing must do what the notes dictate."

WORDS & MUSIC

3-SECOND NOTE
During the Renaissance, music was seen increasingly as a way of achieving expressive communication, clearly projecting the text and stirring the emotions of the listener.

3-MINUTE REFRAIN
One curious type of word painting cultivated in the Renaissance involved devices that were apparent to the performers reading the music, but not to the listener, and exploited some aspect of the musical notation itself to represent the object described. For example, references to the eyes ("occhi" in Italian) of the beloved in the texts of madrigals could be set by composers as two round notes (semibreves) of equal pitch.

In the fifteenth and sixteenth centuries, a growing desire developed to restore the nature and powers of music which classical writers described: music should serve the text, and should have the ability to move the listener through the choice of appropriate musical mode, for example. Such aims reflected a wider emphasis on language and eloquence within Renaissance humanism. Composers matched the accentuation of the text in their musical rhythms, and highlighted particular syllables, words, and phrases by shaping the melodic line, using dissonance or striking harmonies, and manipulating the musical texture. Although the imitative counterpoint, which was commonplace during the period, could sometimes obscure the text—because each voice-part was at a different place in the text at a given point in the music— it brought the advantage that every phrase of text was heard many times, in different voices. Specific ideas in the text could also be reflected through "word painting" (which was particularly common in the Italian madrigal), where the music mimicked the textual concept. The need to make the sung text audible to listeners was emphasized within the Protestant reform movements and the Catholic Counter-Reformation, and music's power of expression was a useful evangelizing tool.

RELATED TOPICS
See also
MASS SETTINGS
page 34

JOSQUIN DESPREZ
page 36

GIOVANNI PIERLUIGI
DA PALESTRINA
page 40

3-SECOND BIOGRAPHIES
GIOSEFFO ZARLINO
1517–90
Italian music theorist, author of an influential set of rules for fitting music and text together

VINCENZO GALILEI
d. 1591
Theorist who argued that vocal counterpoint should be replaced by a single vocal line, following the rhythms of speech

LUCA MARENZIO
1553/4–99
Italian madrigal composer of works notable for their frequent word painting

EXPERT
Owen Rees

Caravaggio depicted a madrigal performance in The Musicians *(top).*

GIOVANNI PIERLUIGI DA PALESTRINA

Giovanni Pierluigi da Palestrina

(c. 1525–94) was a prominent figure in Roman musical culture during a period of upheaval in the Catholic church—the Counter-Reformation—and of expansion in the use of polyphonic music in Rome's churches. He received his training at one of the papal basilicas, Santa Maria Maggiore, and went on to direct the music there and at the other two greatest churches in Rome, St. Peter's and St. John Lateran. In addition, he composed music for the Papal Chapel, Rome's confraternities, and private patrons including the Duke of Mantua. His international fame was boosted considerably through publication of his music in Rome and Venice. Palestrina's prodigious output included more than a hundred Masses and several hundred motets, as well as numerous madrigals (both sacred and secular). The desire for intelligibility of texts sung in polyphony, discussed at the Council of Trent, is manifest in some of Palestrina's works, including sections of the famous *Missa Papæ Marcelli*, but a broader outcome of the Catholic Reformation was renewed emphasis on music's power to encourage devotion. While Palestrina's music came to be associated principally with technical perfection, his output includes powerfully expressive motets on texts from the Song of Songs and dramatic polychoral works.

3-SECOND NOTE
Palestrina's style came to represent the perfection of Renaissance polyphony, and his status benefited from the legend that he prevented the banning of sacred music.

3-MINUTE REFRAIN
Within a few years of Palestrina's death the myth already existed that by composing the *Missa Papæ Marcelli*—so that the text is audible—Palestrina saved church music from a papal ban. The myth survived the centuries, forming the subject of Pfitzner's opera *Palestrina* of 1917. More broadly, Palestrina's music became the principal model for composing in the stile antico, and was at the heart of the nineteenth-century revival in polyphonic sacred music.

RELATED TOPICS
See also
MASS SETTINGS
page 34

JOSQUIN DESPREZ
page 36

WORDS & MUSIC
page 38

3-SECOND BIOGRAPHIES
GIOVANNI MARIA CIOCCHI DEL MONTE
1487–1555
Pope Julius III, the dedicatee of Palestrina's first published book of Masses, who secured for Palestrina a place in the choir of the Sistine Chapel

GUGLIELMO GONZAGA
1538–87
Duke of Mantua who commissioned Masses from Palestrina and sent him his own music for comment

EXPERT
Owen Rees

Palestrina directed the choir at the St. Peter's Basilica in Rome, which was under construction during his lifetime.

1972–5
Peter Phillips (b. 1953) reads Music at Oxford, and is organ scholar at St. John's College

1973
Phillips begins to direct his first concerts of Renaissance sacred polyphony in Oxford

1976
Phillips chooses the name "The Tallis Scholars" for his ensemble, for a concert in the chapel of Winchester College

1980
Peter Phillips and Steve Smith found Gimell Records together

1983
The ensemble takes the financially risky step of turning fully professional

1987
A recording of Masses by Josquin Desprez wins the *Gramophone* Record of the Year award

February 1994
To commemorate the 400th anniversary of Palestrina's death, the ensemble performs in the Basilica di Santa Maria Maggiore, Rome

April 1994
The Tallis Scholars sing Allegri's *Miserere* in the newly restored Sistine Chapel in the Vatican

1998
The Tallis Scholars mark their 25th anniversary with a performance in London's National Gallery

2000
The ensemble performs in New York City alongside Paul McCartney

2015
The Tallis Scholars present their 2,000th concert, in St. John's Smith Square, London

THE TALLIS SCHOLARS

This internationally renowned

British vocal consort is directed by Peter Phillips. It specializes in Renaissance sacred music, performed a cappella, and its distinctive sound and approach are famous through dozens of recordings and thousands of concerts.

Phillips began to direct concerts of Renaissance sacred polyphony while a student at Oxford in 1973, using undergraduate singers. Among those who influenced him as a performer was one of his tutors, David Wulstan, who directed The Clerkes of Oxenford, a group focusing on Tudor polyphony performed with a strikingly pure sound and avoiding what Wulstan thought were tasteless expressive nuances. In 1983, The Tallis Scholars became fully professional and, after their recording of Masses by Josquin Desprez won the *Gramophone* Record of the Year award in 1987, the group developed a busy schedule of international concert tours.

The ensemble's repertoire consists mainly of late-fifteenth- and sixteenth-century sacred polyphony. Given the name of the group, it is unsurprising that they perform a great deal of Tudor music, including many works by English composer Thomas Tallis and his pupil William Byrd. However, they have also recorded pieces by many other composers: from France and the Low Countries (Mouton, Obrecht, Josquin, Gombert, and Clemens non Papa), Italy (Palestrina), Spain (Morales, Guerrero, and Victoria), and Portugal (Cardoso and Lobo). The group has played a major role in bringing unfamiliar repertoire to a wider public, alongside famous sacred masterworks such as Allegri's *Miserere*, Palestrina's *Missa Papæ Marcelli* and Victoria's music for Holy Week.

The Tallis Scholars is a mixed-voice ensemble, typically using ten singers, normally with two singers per part, and performs a cappella. They have cultivated a full, direct, and powerful sound. Phillips likes to present the music they perform in a straightforward manner, aiming to create a "classic" approach to Renaissance polyphony. He emphasizes that his performances and recordings are not driven by the search for historical authenticity or a desire to evoke the liturgical contexts in which sacred music was originally performed, but, instead, by his personal taste and his wish to ensure that Renaissance sacred polyphony appeals to the widest possible audiences.

The Tallis Scholars have also recorded works by some of the most famous contemporary composers of vocal music, including pieces by Arvo Pärt, John Tavener, and Eric Whitacre. The group founded its own associated record label, Gimell Records. This commercial recording aspect of The Tallis Scholars was set up by Steve Smith, who first made a recording of one of the group's concerts in Merton College, Oxford, in 1976, while he was a student of Sound Recording at the University of Surrey. Gimell Records now has a catalog of several dozen recordings by the group.

Owen Rees

HISTORICALLY INFORMED PERFORMANCE

From the 1960s, "authenticity" in performing early music became a widespread and fashionable ideal, but in the 1980s claims that performances could or should be labeled "authentic" began to seem suspect. Since then, the less ambitious expression "historically informed performance" has come into common use. It describes performances reflecting what we can find out about performance conventions of the relevant times, for example by studying or recreating historical instruments, consulting treatises, scrutinizing scores, or researching the size of performing ensembles. Such performances reflect current fascinations with heritage and the vivid recreation of the past, but, ironically, they have also led to the introduction of many sounds and performance styles that are appealingly novel within the world of modern classical music-making. On average, it is more difficult to achieve historically informed performance for Renaissance music than for later repertories, since we have less of the relevant evidence (such as surviving instruments and detailed performance treatises) than we do for Baroque or Classical music. Many professional players now specialize in Renaissance instruments, such as viols, lutes, and cornetts, and vocal ensembles focusing on Renaissance music frequently sing with restricted vibrato and may use period pronunciation of texts.

RELATED TOPICS
See also
EMMA KIRKBY
page 22

THE TALLIS SCHOLARS
page 42

3-SECOND BIOGRAPHIES
ARNOLD DOLMETSCH
1858–1940
French-born instrument-maker and musician, and a pioneering figure in the revival of interest in early instruments and "authentic" ways of performing

JOHN BUTT
1960–
English musicologist, performer, and director whose book *Playing with History* is among the most stimulating discussions of historically informed performance

EXPERT
Owen Rees

The lute has enjoyed a revival as part of the historically informed performance movement.

BAROQUE

basso continuo (Italian: "continuous bass") A system of notation common in Baroque music from around 1600. The composer would write a melody and bassline, but leave the performers to fill in the chords, harmonies, and inner parts. Often composers would also provide numbers above the bassline (known as figured bass) to indicate the intended harmonies. The bassline and chords would be played by "continuo instruments." These weren't always specified, but often included the harpsichord, organ, lute, or low string instruments, such as the bass viol.

cadenza A short section usually found toward the end of a concerto movement (a three to four movement piece for soloist and orchestra) or aria (an operatic solo song). The soloist plays or sings the cadenza unaccompanied or with minimal accompaniment. It allows an opportunity for them to showcase their virtuosity, as cadenzas are usually technically demanding. The cadenza usually ends on a long trill (two neighboring notes alternating quickly) signaling that the orchestra should re-enter. Cadenzas were traditionally improvised, but from the time of Mozart and Beethoven composers have tended to write out cadenzas in full, though performers can still supply their own.

contrapuntal Relating to or following the rules of counterpoint (see below).

counterpoint A type of musical texture involving the sounding of more than one musical voice simultaneously. Each voice is significant in its own right, and counterpoint may involve a number of simultaneous melodic lines. Counterpoint reached its height in the sixteenth and seventeenth centuries, and many textbooks were written during this time setting out strict rules for students.

dissonance Two or more notes played together that produce a discord, which is jarring to the ear. Playing adjacent notes in the scale will produce a dissonance. Traditionally, in classical music dissonances are "resolved" with a consonant chord, which sounds harmonious, stable, and complete. However, dissonance has often been used for expressive reasons, in order to aid expression of madrigal texts. In the nineteenth century composers experimented further with dissonance, introducing new harmonies, and avoiding or prolonging the time until resolution. In the twentieth century many composers were influenced by Schoenberg's idea of the "emancipation of the dissonance," treating traditionally dissonant chords as stable harmonies.

fugue (Italian *fuga*: "flight") A compositional technique. In the first section, or "exposition," a short melodic line, known as a subject, is imitated in successive voices (described thus whether they are instrumental or vocal). When the subject has been heard in all voices a new section (known as an "episode") begins, developing material that has occurred in the exposition and usually modulating to a new key. Then, the subject returns and the rest of the piece consists of alternations between subject entries and episodes.

masque Form of entertainment popular in sixteenth- and seventeenth-century English courts that involved masked dance, poetry, and music.

melismas A decoration commonly found in vocal music in which more than five or six notes are sung per each syllable of text. In plainchant the contrast between melismatic and syllabic (one note per syllable) styles is an important feature. The term can also be used to describe decoration in later music. Melismas can be used to emphasize a particular word in a text or allow a performer to showcase their virtuosity.

monody/monodic A style of accompanied solo singing that came to prominence in the late sixteenth and early seventeenth centuries. A number of different styles of monody developed, including recitative, aria, and madrigal.

prima pratica **and** *seconda pratica* Terms used in the early seventeenth century to differentiate between sixteenth-century vocal polyphony (*prima pratica* or first practice) and a new style emerging with Monteverdi and his contemporaries (*seconda pratica* or second practice). Monteverdi used the term *seconda pratica* when defending his music against criticisms that it broke traditional rules of voice-leading and harmony. He defended these practices by saying they were necessary in order to express the meaning of the text. Earlier styles of polyphony prioritized musical rules over expressive meaning.

word painting A compositional technique in which the composer tries to reflect the meaning of a text in a quite specific, decorative way. For example, if the text referred to climbing, the composer might depict this in a passage of ascending notes. The technique is particularly associated with sixteenth-century madrigals, but can also be found in later Baroque music, and even in the program music of the nineteenth century.

CLAUDIO MONTEVERDI

For 20 years Claudio Monteverdi (1567–1643) worked as court composer to Vincenzo I, in Mantua, but was released by the Duke's successor in 1612; fortunately, he obtained a prestigious position at St. Mark's, Venice, the following year and spent the rest of his life in the city. His output is essentially vocal. Over the course of nine books of madrigals he developed the form from the polyphonic counterpoint of the late Renaissance, which he termed *prima pratica*, to the harmony-and-accompaniment-based Baroque style developing at that time, which he called *seconda pratica*. This style prized the expression of the text, and is noted for freer use of previously banned dissonances for expressive effect. His church music, of which his *Vespers* (1610) form the largest collection, follows a similar pattern; he probably assembled it in the hope of securing a job in Rome. Keenly following the latest trends while surpassing those setting them, he began to compose in the new form of opera at the Mantuan court, where *Orfeo* premiered in 1607; three decades later, after the world's first public opera houses had opened in Venice, he composed further operatic works, of which *Il ritorno d'Ulisse in patria* and *L'incoronazione di Poppea* survive.

RELATED TOPICS

See also

WORDS & MUSIC
page 38

HISTORICALLY INFORMED PERFORMANCE
page 44

THE ENGLISH BAROQUE
page 52

3-SECOND BIOGRAPHIES

GIOVANNI ARTUSI
c. 1540–1613
Italian theorist who, in 1600–3, attacked Monteverdi's use of dissonance in his madrigals

CATERINA MARTINELLI
1589/90–1608
Italian soprano who died of smallpox before she could play the title role in Monteverdi's now largely lost opera *Arianna*

GIOVANNI BUSENELLO
1598–1659
Venetian librettist of *Poppea*, Monteverdi's last opera, based on ancient Roman history

EXPERT
George Hall

Monteverdi spent his career in Venice after moving there in 1613.

THE ENGLISH BAROQUE

3-SECOND NOTE
The Baroque arrived later in England than in France or Germany, partly owing to the interruption in musical life caused by the English Civil War.

3-MINUTE REFRAIN
Henry Purcell (1659–95) was the greatest of English Baroque composers, writing in all available forms for court, church, and theater. His father was a member of the Chapel Royal, which he himself joined as a child chorister, studying under Humfrey and Blow. Purcell's obvious talent saw him engaging with London's musical life at the highest level, writing odes for court occasions, anthems for Westminster Abbey, and semi-operas for Dorset Garden and Drury Lane.

Baroque's full impact was only felt in England following the Restoration in 1660, when Charles II assumed the throne, bringing along with him musical tastes formed during his time at the French court. Consequently, young musicians such as Pelham Humfrey were sent to France to acquire the latest techniques, returning in his case, in the diarist Samuel Pepys' words, "an absolute monsieur as full of form and confidence and vanity, and disparages everyone's skill but his own." The result was that from the outset English Baroque music, best exemplified in the works of Purcell, combined elements of Italian Baroque and its French derivative together with conservative native traits that lingered from an earlier age, including simple solos and choruses in the style of tuneful English airs and a use of dance inherited from the masque tradition. Opera took off slowly, partly due to the closing of the theaters by the Puritans in the Civil War; for decades London opera-goers favored a mixed-genre approach known as semi-opera or "dramatick opera," in which spoken dialog was interspersed with masque-like musical sections. Only in 1710, with the arrival of German-born, Italian-trained George Frideric Handel in London were regular Italian opera seasons instigated; he also introduced to England the sacred form of oratorio.

RELATED TOPICS
See also
GEORGE FRIDERIC HANDEL
page 58

ORATORIO
page 60

3-SECOND BIOGRAPHIES
SAMUEL PEPYS
1633–1703
English naval administrator and MP whose diary (1660–69) provides commentary on English musical and theatrical life

PELHAM HUMFREY
1647–74
English composer sent to France by Charles II to learn the latest French musical fashions, which he passed on to his pupil Henry Purcell

JOHN BLOW
1649–1708
English composer and teacher of Purcell; his only opera, *Venus and Adonis*, influenced Purcell's *Dido and Aeneas*

EXPERT
George Hall

Charles II would have heard church music by Purcell in the Chapel Royal at Hampton Court Palace.

sing and not for a pain Love was made for a Blef- - -

Blessing was made for a   Blessing and not for a pain   Love was made for a

ANTONIO VIVALDI

Spending most of his career

in his native Venice, Vivaldi (1678–1741) spent much of his time in the city training the inhabitants of the Ospedale della Pietà, a female orphanage where the girls and women earned their keep by giving concerts to a standard that won the admiration of sophisticated foreign visitors. Most of his instrumental and choral music was produced for these performers. His concertos alone—many for the violin (which he played to a virtuoso standard), but also numerous examples for other instruments, and some for two or more instruments together—number 500. While Stravinsky's quip that Vivaldi composed the same concerto 500 times may be funny, it's hardly fair; his orchestral compositions show consistent inventiveness. Vivaldi was also a notable exponent of the sonata—an instrumental piece in several movements usually (in his case) written for one or two violins plus basso continuo. From 1713 onward he became involved in opera as both composer and manager, writing some 50 examples in all. In 1740, aged 62, he traveled to Vienna, perhaps hoping to produce opera there or gain permanent employment under the Emperor Charles VI; but the latter died suddenly, and Vivaldi, reduced to poverty, followed suit nine months later.

3-SECOND NOTE
Like many Baroque composers Vivaldi was both influential and extremely prolific: his music traveled around Europe and gained the admiration of J. S. Bach.

3-MINUTE REFRAIN
The Four Seasons are violin concertos describing the sounds of and feelings inspired by spring, summer, fall, and winter; they open a larger collection of 12 entitled *Il cimento dell'armonia e dell'invenzione* ("The Contest Between Harmony and Invention"), published in Amsterdam in 1725. Forgotten—like all of Vivaldi's music—after the composer's death, they were rediscovered in the twentieth century and first recorded around 1940; since then more than one thousand alternatives have been issued.

RELATED TOPICS
See also
HISTORICALLY INFORMED PERFORMANCE
page 44

NIGEL KENNEDY
page 56

PATRONAGE
page 70

3-SECOND BIOGRAPHIES
BENEDETTO MARCELLO
1686–1739
Fellow Venetian who published *Il teatro alla moda*, a waspish pamphlet satirizing the operatic world and referring to Vivaldi by anagrammatic pseudonym Aldiviva Licante

ANNA GIRÒ (GIRAUD)
c. 1710–c. 1747
Italian mezzo-soprano who starred in Vivaldi's operas and was both his pupil and traveling companion

EXPERT
George Hall

Antonio Vivaldi's career was focused on the Ospedale della Pietà in Venice.

Del Sig: D. Antonio Vivaldi

1956
Born in Brighton, UK

1963
Studies at the Yehudi
Menuhin School of Music

1977
Makes his Royal Festival
Hall debut with the
Mendelssohn concerto
under Riccardo Muti

1984
His recording of Elgar's
Violin Concerto
establishes him as an
outstanding violinist

1989
His recording of *The Four
Seasons* is released

1991
Publishes autobiography,
Always Playing

1997
Returns to classical music
after a five-year gap

2000
Joins The Who for a gig
at the Royal Albert Hall

2005
Records a jazz album for
the Blue Note Sessions
label

2008
Returning to the BBC
Proms for the first time
in 11 years, he plays Elgar
and a jazz program
accompanied by the
Nigel Kennedy Quintet

2013
His controversial remarks
during a Prom featuring
Palestinian performers
are edited out of the
television broadcast

NIGEL KENNEDY

One of the most gifted violinists of his generation, Nigel Kennedy has moved in and out of the world of classical music, freely exploring other genres and finding either himself or his recreated image arguably more at home in the alternative worlds of jazz and pop.

Born to a family of musicians in Brighton, England, in 1956, he showed a keen interest in music from an early age and initially took piano lessons from his mother: she and his cellist father had divorced and the latter had returned to Australia, where he had grown up. Meanwhile, Nigel began serious musical training as a violinist at the Yehudi Menuhin School of Music aged seven; subsequently he would study at the Juilliard in New York with the famous teacher Dorothy DeLay.

His parallel interest in jazz—inspired as a child by his stepfather's Fats Waller records—was reignited when the French jazz violinist Stéphane Grappelli invited Kennedy, aged 16, to appear with him at Carnegie Hall.

In 1984, his first recording of Elgar's Violin Concerto was well received; however, some of his later concerto recordings have been criticized for including his own, stylistically incongruous cadenzas.

Released in 1989 and selling more than two million copies, his first version of Vivaldi's *The Four Seasons* established him as a media celebrity. Interviews and other subsequent self-publicity, however, have aroused a mixed response. Kennedy—for a while he asked to be referred to only by his surname—now spoke with a self-consciously streetwise accent and vocabulary; describing the result as "Mockney," some commentators found his new image phoney and rather embarrassing, while for others it represented an endearing and much-needed loosening-up of the formality of classical music.

Yet with a public image that repelled as much as it attracted, plus outspoken views on the classical world and even politics (a brief comment suggesting that Israel practiced apartheid was edited out of a BBC Proms television broadcast in 2013), Kennedy's unconventional behavior has sometimes masked the genuine power of his actual music-making.

Collaborations with The Who, Kate Bush, Sarah Brightman, and Boy George have alternated—sometimes with long intervals in between—with performances and recordings of works by Bach and the other great classical composers, including new versions of both his iconic *Elgar* (1997) and *Vivaldi* (2015) disks. In spite of his controversial image, there is not nearly so much of a divide in opinion about his musicianship itself: Kennedy is regularly a spellbinding performer.

George Hall

GEORGE FRIDERIC HANDEL

RELATED TOPICS
See also
ORATORIO
page 60

JOHANN SEBASTIAN BACH
page 62

JOSEPH HAYDN
page 72

FELIX MENDELSSOHN
page 92

3-SECOND NOTE

German-born, but later a naturalized British subject, Handel was a prolific and highly influential composer, particularly of opera and large-scale vocal works.

3-MINUTE REFRAIN

Handel was an important supporter of several major charitable enterprises: he helped to establish the Fund for the Support of Decay'd Musicians (now the Royal Society of Musicians), and later became a governor of the Foundling Hospital in London. For this organization he provided an anthem, *Blessed are They that Considereth the Poor*, and directed annual benefit performances of *Messiah*, the score and parts of which he left to the Hospital in his will.

In a varied and highly successful career Handel (1685–1759) went from early positions in northern Germany to Italy in 1706 and, later, to London. Italian opera was an enormously popular and successful musical form in England, and Handel's operatic works combine the color and lyricism of Italian writing with French dance forms, English choral style, and German harmony and counterpoint. Traveling extensively around Germany, Italy, and Britain, he entered the employ of the British monarchy in 1713, eventually settling in England. His most successful operas include *Rinaldo* (1711; his major breakthrough onto the London scene), *Giulio Cesare in Egitto* (1724), and *Alcina* and *Ariodante* (1735), and he was involved in the business and organization of operatic seasons as well as providing and directing the music. He also composed several pieces for the royal family, famously the so-called "Coronation" anthems for George II, and "Music for the Royal Fireworks" in 1749. In later years he turned from opera to oratorio, bringing unprecedented drama and musical characterization to biblical narratives. *Saul, Israel in Egypt,* and, most importantly, *Messiah* were rapturously received at the time, and remained hugely popular throughout the later eighteenth and nineteenth centuries, inspiring Haydn, Mendelssohn, and others.

3-SECOND BIOGRAPHIES
FRIEDRICH ZACHOW
1663–1712
German composer and organist. He was Handel's first teacher, instructing him in composition, organ, and harpsichord

KING GEORGE II
1683–1760
German-born ruler of Great Britain (1727–60). Handel worked briefly for George II while he was a prince in Hanover; and went on to compose for his coronation.

EXPERT
Katy Hamilton

Handel's "Music for the Royal Fireworks" required more than 50 wind and brass players.

George Frideric Handel

ORATORIO

Oratorios arose in seventeenth-century Italy as a substitute for opera during Lent, when opera houses were perforce closed. Their texts, intended to enforce important religious lessons, treated biblical or, at least ethical, subjects, such as the lives of saints. The original performance venue was the church prayer hall, or "oratorio," which became eponymous with the genre itself. In the eighteenth century, the huge success of Handel's oratorios, with their colorfully dramatic choruses, set the scene for even greater popularity in the nineteenth, in Britain especially, where the establishing of numerous choral societies and music festivals stimulated the composition of new oratorios and the revival of old, usually with preposterously expanded forces. The latter tendency culminated in performances of Handel's oratorios in London's Crystal Palace in the 1880s with some 450 instrumentalists and 4,000 singers—more than ten times the numbers at the 1742 premiere of *Messiah*. Oratorio enjoyed great popularity until the early 1900s, when a lessening of religious fervor and waning enthusiasm for the choral societies that provided most of its singers caused significant decline. Nevertheless, certain oratorios remain firmly in the standard repertoire, including Handel's *Messiah*, Mendelssohn's *Elijah*, and Elgar's *Dream of Gerontius*.

3-SECOND NOTE
Often defined as the "antithesis" to opera, oratorios are religious compositions for soloists, chorus, and orchestra, featuring narrative, dramatic, and contemplative elements, but without the assistance of scenery, costume, or action.

3-MINUTE REFRAIN
The distinction between oratorio and opera seems clear by most definitions, but there are many "crossover" works: sacred operas (Saint-Saens' *Samson and Delilah*), secular oratorios (Schumann's *Paradise and the Peri*), and oratorios with a long history of operatic stage performance (Liszt's *St. Elizabeth*). Fundamental differences are that oratorios were usually performed in the audience's native language, and that the genre attracted amateur performers as much as professional ensembles.

RELATED TOPICS
See also
WORDS & MUSIC
page 38

GEORGE FRIDERIC HANDEL
page 58

FELIX MENDELSSOHN
page 92

FRANZ LISZT
page 100

3-SECOND BIOGRAPHIES
EMILIO DE' CAVALIERI
c. 1550–1602
Italian composer of what is often considered the earliest surviving oratorio, *Rappresentatione di Anima e di Corpo* (1600)

GIACOMO CARISSIMI
1605–74
Italian composer notable for secular cantatas and for 16 oratorios (in Latin) in which his characters express emotions during breaks in the narrative, as in opera

EXPERT
Monika Hennemann

Handel's Messiah *is one of the best-known and most frequently performed oratorios.*

JOHANN SEBASTIAN BACH

RELATED TOPICS
See also
HISTORICALLY INFORMED
PERFORMANCE
page 44

GEORGE FRIDERIC HANDEL
page 58

PATRONAGE
page 70

FELIX MENDELSSOHN
page 92

Most closely associated with the city of Leipzig, Bach (1685–1750) worked at the Thomaskirche in the city from 1723. Earlier, he held posts in several other cities (unlike Handel, he never traveled beyond Germany), and his musical duties in these jobs account for his substantial output, particularly of sacred cantatas. Many of his most important instrumental pieces, including *The Well-Tempered Clavier*, the Suites for Cello, the Sonatas and Partitas for violin, and the Brandenburg Concertos, were completed in Cöthen in the 1720s; these works all serve to explore the potential of the instruments involved, probably based on Bach's exchanges with noted players of the day, and his own considerable abilities as a violinist and keyboardist. The St. Matthew and St. John Passions, both composed in Leipzig, unite biblical excerpts and literary texts and also involve well-known chorales. His genius as a contrapuntalist is most apparent in *The Well-Tempered Clavier*, numerous organ compositions, and the *Art of Fugue*, completed in the 1740s. The intricacy and intellectualism of his approach is balanced by fine attention to instrumental color, melody, and dramatic pacing, all crucial features of his vocal, as well as instrumental, works.

3-SECOND NOTE
Most famous during his lifetime as a performer, Bach's compositional legacy—particularly his contrapuntal writing—had a profound and enduring influence on Western music, one that ensured his reputation posthumously.

3-MINUTE REFRAIN
By the 1740s, Bach's music was considered stylistically outdated. It was superseded by the simpler, non-contrapuntal approaches of the next generation, including several of his sons (notably C. P. E. Bach and J. C. Bach). In the early 1800s, composers such as Beethoven and Mendelssohn "rediscovered" Bach's music—he became the first musical figure to receive scholarly attention in the very earliest days of musicological research. A complete edition of his music was issued between 1850 and 1899.

3-SECOND BIOGRAPHIES
CARL PHILIPP EMANUEL BACH
1714–88
Bach's second son, and one of the most important German composers of the later 1700s

JOHANN CHRISTIAN BACH
1735–82
Bach's youngest son, who spent 20 years of his career in London and was a driving force behind the establishment of public concerts in the capital

EXPERT
Katy Hamilton

Bach composed more than 200 cantatas, a Mass in B minor, and many other sacred works.

Johann Sebastian Bach.

CLASSICAL

CLASSICAL
GLOSSARY

canon (Latin: "rule") A type of musical imitation in which all voices sing or play exactly the same melody, but enter after different intervals of time.

cross-stringing A term (sometimes called "overstringing") referring to the way the strings of a piano are arranged in two parallel planes passing diagonally over one another. It was common in pianos from the nineteenth century, supplanting "straight-stringing" in which the strings are perpendicular and do not overlap. Cross-stringing produces a more resonant sound, particularly in the bass of the piano, but it has also been criticized for producing a more blended, murky sound.

dynamics Instructions that indicate to performers the volume at which the music should be played. The most common are the Italian terms *piano* (often abbreviated on the musical score to *p*), meaning soft, and *forte* (*f*) meaning loud.

fugue (Italian *fuga*: "flight") A compositional technique. In the first section, or "exposition," a short melodic line, known as a subject, is imitated in successive voices (described thus whether they are instrumental or vocal). When the subject has been heard in all voices a new section (known as an "episode") begins, developing material that has occurred in the exposition and usually modulating to a new key. Then the subject returns and the rest of the piece consists of alternations between subject entries and episodes.

minuet A stately French dance in triple time (three beats in a bar) that was popular in courts from the 1660s. The minuet also became popular as a movement in instrumental music. It often appears alongside other dances in Baroque suites by composers such as Corelli, Handel, and Purcell. In the eighteenth century it became common to incorporate a minuet as the third movement in four-movement symphonies, string quartets, and sonatas. Minuets provided some relief between the slow second movement and the exciting finale. From Beethoven's symphonies onward, the minuet movement began to be replaced by a scherzo. Minuets are often paired with trios: a second dance in a contrasting key characteristically using woodwind instruments and light textures.

scherzo (Italian: "joke") A lively, fast-paced movement in orchestral music. From Beethoven's symphonies onward, scherzos replaced minuets as the common choice for the third movements of symphonies and string quartets. Like minuets, scherzos are usually in triple time. The term may mean "joke" but the humor often seems savage rather than lighthearted.

sonata form An important musical form that reached prominence in the classical symphony and continued to be widely used and expanded in the nineteenth century. The first movements of symphonies, sonatas, and concertos are often written in the sonata form. Traditionally, this form involves a section called the "exposition" in which the composer sets out two themes in contrasting keys, and usually of contrasting character. In the middle section (the "development"), the composer develops these themes, combining them in new ways, transforming and fragmenting them. In the final section (the "recapitulation"), the composer reintroduces the themes from the exposition and "resolves" the contrasting theme in the same key as the first theme. In classical symphonies, the recapitulation often repeats the exposition literally (apart from changing the key of the second theme). Later, composers began to write longer developments, became more experimental in using key relationships, and sometimes included further development in the recapitulation, alongside a long closing section, or "coda."

timbre The quality or character of the sound of a particular instrument or voice or combination of instruments and/or voices.

WOLFGANG AMADEUS MOZART

3-SECOND NOTE
Together with Bach and Beethoven, Mozart is regarded as one of the quintessentially canonical composers of Western art music.

3-MINUTE REFRAIN
Mozart was a child prodigy whose father took him on tour around the principal European courts, where he played the violin and piano and showcased his juvenile compositions. He is forever associated with his birth town of Salzburg but found musical opportunities there limiting and relocated to Vienna in adult life, although he continued to travel. Mozart moved in important Viennese musical circles and enjoyed the support of fellow freemasons, but he also struggled to manage his financial affairs.

The Austrian composer Wolfgang Amadeus Mozart (1756–1791) wrote an astonishing amount of music in his short lifetime. His compositions are typical of the Classical style, which is characterized by balanced phrase lengths, a clear texture of melody plus accompaniment, and a simpler harmonic language than had been typical of Baroque music. Mozart used sonata form—which embodies the Classical style's emphasis upon musical symmetry—as the underpinning basis for many different types of musical work. He mastered all of the major musical genres of his era: large-scale orchestral works, chamber music, solo instrumental works, choral music, serious and comic opera in the Italian style, and the new, populist German *Singspiel*, as exemplified respectively by his works *Idomeneo*, *Le nozze di Figaro,* and *Die Zauberflöte*. Mozart's sophisticated and original musical characterization, even when working in convention-bound genres, guaranteed his operas a lasting place in the repertory. Mozart died at the age of 35 while working on one of his most famous sacred works, the *Requiem*, whose anonymous commission has become the stuff of legend.

RELATED TOPICS
See also
PATRONAGE
page 70

CHAMBER MUSIC
page 74

THE SYMPHONY
page 76

3-SECOND BIOGRAPHY
ALFRED BRENDEL
1931–
Austrian pianist known for his masterly interpretations of Mozart, among others

EXPERT
Alexandra Wilson

Accomplished in all genres, Mozart created a musical language that is instantly recognizable.

PATRONAGE

RELATED TOPICS
See also
SALON CULTURE
page 94

THE CONCERT HALL
page 120

The Renaissance witnessed the emergence of the first "professional" composers, but at this time they were essentially servants, typically employed by a church, a court, or a nobleman and writing to demand. Thomas Tallis, for example, had to adjust the style of his sacred writing depending upon the faith of the prevailing Tudor monarch. During the Baroque, Bach's position as Cantor at Leipzig's Thomasschule involved composing large quantities of music for local churches and training choristers. The Classical era marked an important turning point in the shift from private to public patronage. Haydn was employed by the wealthy Esterházys: He had to write for the Prince's orchestra, albeit with considerable artistic freedom. By contrast, Mozart struggled to establish a career as a largely freelance composer in Vienna. Composers needed a sound business acumen in order to survive. Beethoven was a transitional figure, still working for individual aristocratic patrons but also negotiating good fees for his music from publishers. By the nineteenth century few aristocrats could afford to employ full-time musicians, but the decline of private patronage was artistically liberating for composers. The Romantic era constructed composers as genius figures rather than as simple craftsmen.

3-SECOND NOTE
Composition is often romanticized as an activity detached from worldly concerns, but economic factors have had a direct impact on the music composers have written.

3-MINUTE REFRAIN
The rise of the middle classes in the nineteenth century led to a thriving concert culture and much domestic music-making. Composers adapted their music to the demands of an expanded public and profited from new opportunities to make money from teaching and sheet-music sales. Patronage may not be so obvious in contemporary society, but somebody is still usually holding the musical purse strings, be it a broadcaster, a movie studio, or a university.

3-SECOND BIOGRAPHIES
ESTERHÁZY FAMILY
fl. 14th–19th centuries
Aristocratic Hungarian dynasty that included many patrons of the arts

THOMAS TALLIS
c. 1505–85
English composer particularly associated with choral music

EXPERT
Alexandra Wilson

Thomas Tallis was forced by traditional court patronage to be one of the most adaptable composers.

JOSEPH HAYDN

RELATED TOPICS
See also
PATRONAGE
page 70

CHAMBER MUSIC
page 74

THE SYMPHONY
page 76

LUDWIG VAN BEETHOVEN
page 78

3-SECOND NOTE
Regarded as the father of both the symphony and the string quartet, Haydn was a prolific composer (he wrote 106 symphonies) and a significant model for Beethoven.

3-MINUTE REFRAIN
Haydn is famous not only as a composer and teacher—most notably of Beethoven—but also as a kind, devout man with a warm sense of humor. Witty compositions such as the *Surprise* and *Farewell* Symphonies (in which the players gradually leave over the course of the finale) are a testament to his humor and musical ingenuity.

Austrian composer Joseph Haydn (1732–1809) spent the majority of his career working for the Esterházy family, high-ranking Hungarian nobles with several country estates as well as links to Vienna. Almost all the music he wrote before the 1780s was for the personal use of the family, and included many dramatic works, operas, and symphonies. In the 1780s, he refined and developed the string quartet into the genre we now recognize—four solo instruments playing four intricate movements—and turned his attention to keyboard trios and sonatas explicitly intended for the new pianoforte, rather than the older harpsichord. Despite sticking to clear musical structures, such as sonata form and rondo, Haydn's chamber works explore a wide range of harmonies, textures, and thematic devices to provide variety and characterization. Similarly, his symphonies are very varied in terms of musical approach and orchestration. Haydn's visits to London in 1791–95 also provided him with the opportunity to write for public concerts, rather than simply private salons. This encouraged more expansive, rhetorical works designed for larger audiences. As a result, both the string quartet and the symphony grew in scale and complexity, and he was inspired to compose oratorios, *The Creation* and *The Seasons* at the turn of the century.

3-SECOND BIOGRAPHIES
ESTERHÁZY FAMILY
fl. 14th–19th centuries
Aristocratic Hungarian dynasty that included many patrons of the arts; Haydn worked for four generations of Esterházys

JOHANN PETER SALOMON
1745–1815
German performer and impresario who settled in London in the 1780s and was instrumental in persuading Haydn to visit England

EXPERT
Katy Hamilton

A devout Catholic, Haydn often wrote Laus Deo—"Praise be to God"—at the end of his manuscripts.

CHAMBER MUSIC

3-SECOND NOTE
Originally defined as music written for performance in a chamber—a limited space and thus for a small number of players—although later, chamber music also featured in public concert venues.

3-MINUTE REFRAIN
In the nineteenth century, the phenomenon of the "public chamber concert" became common across Europe. Composers responded by writing longer, larger-scale pieces with richer, denser musical textures. Some works also used larger ensembles—such as Beethoven's Septet for Winds and Strings (1799), Mendelssohn's String Octet (1825), and Brahms' string sextets (1860 and 1865).

The term "chamber music" was first used in the sixteenth century, and carried with it implications of music for a small ensemble, suitable for performance in private homes—particularly of royalty, the nobility, and the wealthy. By the eighteenth century, chamber music predominantly applied to instrumental compositions and, being written for a private, well-educated audience, it was also considered to be a sophisticated and intimate medium. Listeners could be expected to recognize standard formal types—the sonata form of a string quartet movement, for instance—and thus understand the ingenuity and wit of composers who stretched or broke the rules, such as Mozart and Haydn. Common chamber genres of the later eighteenth century included string trios, quartets and quintets, piano trios, and accompanied sonatas, as well as some small-scale vocal music. Haydn's visits to England in the 1790s were to have a major impact on the development of continental chamber music. In Britain, such music was already being included in large-scale public concerts. Haydn's string quartets, composed for London audiences, employed greater rhetoric, drama, and broader musical textures to suit their new surroundings. This pushed the genre into the public domain, for a wider audience beyond noble connoisseurs.

RELATED TOPICS
See also
WOLFGANG AMADEUS MOZART
page 68

JOSEPH HAYDN
page 72

LUDWIG VAN BEETHOVEN
page 78

FELIX MENDELSSOHN
page 92

3-SECOND BIOGRAPHIES
FRANZ SCHUBERT
1797–1828
Austrian composer who wrote string quartets, piano trios, a piano quintet, and a string quintet; several include direct quotations of his Lieder

ANTONÍN DVOŘÁK
1841–1904
Czech composer who wrote 14 string quartets as well as chamber music with piano

EXPERT
Katy Hamilton

Beethoven's late chamber music was so complex that listeners used miniature scores to follow the performances.

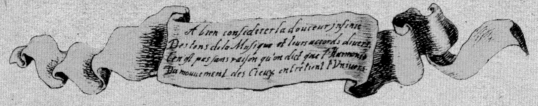

A bien considerer la douceur infinie
Des sons de la Musique et leurs accords divers
Cen est pas sans raison qu'on dict que l'Harmonie
Du mouvement des Cieux entretient l'Univers

THE SYMPHONY

The symphony is an instrumental genre for full orchestra. Its predecessors include the Italian opera overture, the sonata, and the concerto. The earliest concert symphonies were written in three movements (fast-slow-fast) for strings alone. Gradually, the orchestra expanded to include woodwind, brass, and percussion, culminating in the enormous orchestral forces required by Mahler's Symphony No. 8 (dubbed "Symphony of a Thousand") at the turn of the twentieth century. As new instruments were introduced during the nineteenth century, composers such as Berlioz experimented with instrumental colors, developing their own distinctive timbres. The scale of the symphony also expanded to include a minuet and trio movement or scherzo after the slow second movement. Increasingly, movements themselves also became longer, with slow introductions generally preceding the first movement, which was typically in sonata form. The symphony grew in prominence through the eighteenth century, and by the nineteenth century it had become the most prestigious and aesthetically important instrumental genre. Uniting the widest possible range of instruments with no one voice predominating and performed in a large public space, the symphony came to be perceived as an expression of communal sentiment or the universality of humanity.

3-SECOND NOTE
At its high point, the symphony was seen as the most important instrumental genre, but its fortunes have changed over time.

3-MINUTE REFRAIN
Many composers felt that Beethoven had developed the symphony as far as possible. From the 1830s, several turned to other instrumental genres, such as the concert overture or symphonic poem. However, Brahms' symphonies in the 1870s saw the genre revived. The most notable symphonists of the late nineteenth and twentieth centuries include Sibelius, Nielsen, Stravinsky, Elgar, Copland, Vaughan Williams, Shostakovich, and Tippett. After the Second World War, the symphony's traditional preoccupations were seen as irrelevant and many significant composers neglected the genre.

RELATED TOPICS
See also
JOSEPH HAYDN
page 72

LUWIG VAN BEETHOVEN
page 78

THE ORCHESTRA
page 106

THE CONCERT HALL
page 120

3-SECOND BIOGRAPHIES
JOHANN STAMITZ
1717–57
Czech leader of the Mannheim Orchestra; the first symphony composer to use consistently what would become the standard four-movement symphonic model

JEAN SIBELIUS
1865–1957
Finnish composer of symphonies experimenting with dissonances, compression of motivic material, and innovative forms

EXPERT
Joanne Cormac

The scope and originality of Beethoven's nine symphonies redefined the genre.

LUDWIG VAN BEETHOVEN

3-SECOND NOTE

Musical innovator, political thinker, and pioneering "Romantic," Beethoven's vocal, dramatic, and, above all, instrumental compositions revolutionized musical thinking, and have remained enormously influential ever since.

3-MINUTE REFRAIN

The extent to which Beethoven reconceived and individuated musical genres made him a tour de force for subsequent generations who felt they needed to surpass his works in some way in order to be original. This, combined with elements of his biography—particularly his deafness and his mysterious "Immortal Beloved"—have earned Beethoven legendary status as a tortured Romantic genius. He has come to stand, in the popular imagination, for all classical music.

A prodigiously talented pianist and ambitious composer, Beethoven (1770–1827) moved from his hometown, Bonn, to Vienna in 1792 and studied briefly with Haydn and Salieri. Even his earliest works deliberately subverted the musical conventions of Haydn and Mozart; he remained a great innovator throughout his life. He found new ways to develop established musical forms, incorporating unusual key relations, expanding structures—even linking movements of a work through a single unifying motive in the Fifth Symphony. In his later compositions, Beethoven also incorporated Baroque models, using fugues in many of his piano sonatas and string quartets. Born into the age of early Romanticism, his music also displays new aesthetic and philosophical ideas. Unlike his predecessors, he composed far fewer pieces in major genres—symphonies, operas, string quartets, and piano sonatas—since originality was becoming an increasingly important marker of artistic eminence. His Third Symphony, a tribute to Napoleon, traces a philosophical journey of heroic greatness; the Sixth includes descriptive titles that profoundly influenced the subsequent development of program music; and the Ninth breaks the symphonic mould by incorporating voices. Such radical innovations earned him fame across Europe and beyond.

RELATED TOPICS

See also
CHAMBER MUSIC
page 74

THE SYMPHONY
page 76

THE PIANO
page 82

PROGRAM MUSIC
page 98

3-SECOND BIOGRAPHIES

ANTONIO SALIERI
1750–1825
Italian composer associated with Vienna where he was Court Music Director and a teacher of young musicians

"IMMORTAL BELOVED"
The addressee of a famous letter from Beethoven, most likely a woman unable to reciprocate his love due to circumstance; she may have been married aristocrat Antonie Brentano (1780–1869)

EXPERT

Katy Hamilton

Beethoven's admiration for Napoleon ended when he was declared Emperor of France.

L. van BEETHOVEN.

Arrangement

für das Pianoforte zu vier Händen.

1819
Born in Leipzig

1824
Begins piano lessons with her father

1830
Debut at Leipzig Gewandhaus

1831
Tour of Paris with Wieck

1835
Robert and Clara begin their courtship

1837
Concert tour of Vienna. Clara named Royal and Imperial Virtuosa

1840
Marriage of Robert and Clara

1841
Birth of first child, Marie

1844
Concert tour to Russia with Robert

1853
Meets Brahms

1854
Robert attempts suicide and is hospitalized

1855
Clara begins touring again

1856
Tours to Vienna, Prague, Budapest, and England; Robert Schumann dies

1870
Clara's son Ludwig is institutionalized

1872
Death of daughter, Julie

1877
Begins editing Schumann's works

1888
Celebrates 80th jubilee as concert artist

1891
Final public concert, Frankfurt

1896
Dies of a stroke

CLARA SCHUMANN

Clara Schumann (née Wieck) was one of the most acclaimed virtuoso pianists of her day. Married to the composer Robert Schumann, Clara was a highly skilled musician in her own right, and was also a composer, editor, and teacher.

Clara began piano lessons aged five, taught by her father, Friedrich Wieck. Unusually for the time, Wieck never saw Clara's gender as a barrier to a successful career, encouraging her to tour and compose. However, Wieck was also domineering and controlling. Not only did Wieck read all of Clara's diary entries, he even wrote some himself, using the first person, as if it were Clara writing.

Clara achieved success at a young age, undertaking highly successful and demanding tours of Europe. Wieck accompanied Clara on the majority of the tours from 1828 to 1840, acting as both her manager and publicist. Wieck's support of his daughter was also exploitative; he kept the large sums of money she earned from her performances. At first Clara did not question this, but when she was older she requested her money. Wieck claimed that the money was rightfully his because he had taught her to play.

Wieck violently opposed the relationship between Clara and his pupil Robert Schumann, even bringing court actions against them. Clara found it difficult to oppose Wieck, who had been so influential, but eventually the couple defied him and married. They had a loving marriage, but it was marked by tragedy. Robert suffered from an undiagnosed mental illness, which worsened in time. He attempted suicide in 1854 and was soon after hospitalized, dying in the hospital in 1856.

Following Robert's death, Clara bore the sole responsibility for supporting herself and the couple's eight children. She had toured less frequently once married to Robert (and had missed it terribly), but now began again in earnest. Clara's playing was noted for its excellent technique, warmth, sincerity, and rich tone. Above all, she valued the intentions of the composer. In this she was forward-thinking, as at the time many performers freely embellished musical works as they saw fit. Clara also composed piano pieces and songs. Her most admired work is her piano trio (*Opus 17*), which demonstrates skilled handling of material across a large-scale work. She stopped composing after Robert's death, and always lacked confidence in composition, seeing herself first and foremost as a performer. She never stopped promoting Robert's works through her performances and the collected editions which she prepared.

Joanne Cormac

THE PIANO

The piano was created around 1700 by Bartolomeo Cristofori, whose intention was to produce "a harpsichord capable of both soft (*piano*) and loud (*forte*) notes"—hence the designation "pianoforte." The instrument he eventually invented produced its sound by hitting the strings with hammers operated from a keyboard, rather than by plucking the strings like a harpsichord. It was this hammer stroke, however, that allowed dynamic variety. Cristofori's genius lay in devising an action that would prompt the hammer quickly to strike the string, and then immediately fall back, allowing the note to ring until the string was damped. Nevertheless, Cristofori's piano did not have a mechanism that allowed all the dampers to be raised at once to produce a more singing tone. This indispensable innovation was later added by Gottfried Silbermann. The further inventions of a much improved action by Sébastien Érard in 1821, of a complete iron frame by Jonas Chickering in 1843, and the popularization of cross-strung pianos by Steinway from 1859, largely completed the march to the modern instrument, while virtuosi like Franz Liszt, Anton Rubinstein, and Ignacy Paderewski ensured the piano's place as the premier solo concert instrument from the Romantic era to the present day.

RELATED TOPICS
See also
FRANZ LISZT
page 100

VIRTUOSITY
page 102

3-SECOND NOTE
The piano is one of the most versatile musical instruments, dominating Western domestic music-making for more than two centuries, and of continuing crucial importance in concert life.

3-MINUTE REFRAIN
The key to the piano's popularity is its ability to allow a single musician to produce both melody and harmony, to imitate both voices and orchestra. As a result, it became for the concert hall the Romantic solo instrument par excellence, feeding equally the egos of the performers and the audiences' desires, as well as providing the ultimate symbol of bourgeois respectability for the middle-class parlor.

3-SECOND BIOGRAPHIES
ANTON RUBINSTEIN
1829–94
Russian composer and premier pianist of the generation after Liszt; although a somewhat mediocre composer, Rubinstein's powerful performance style indelibly influenced younger artists such as Ignacy Paderewski and Ferruccio Busoni

IGNACY PADEREWSKI
1860–1941
Polish politician, patriot, and the highest-paid pianist of all time, famous for his singing tone and uniquely authoritative performances, and one of the first to achieve equal success as a recording artist

EXPERT
Kenneth Hamilton

Cristofori's piano action (left) and a modern version (right). Despite some differences, the principle is the same.

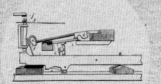
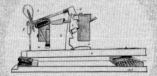

THE NINETEENTH CENTURY

absolute music In contrast to program music, absolute music is not intended to represent an extra-musical subject, such as a poem or painting or even an emotion. Instead, the music is considered to be abstract and autonomous. Absolute music does not contain words, as a text would lend a representational quality to the music, so the term usually refers to instrumental rather than vocal music.

figuration A term often used to describe passagework or accompaniment with a distinctive and easily identifiable, repeated shape, such as an arpeggio.

idée fixe (French: "obsession") A term coined by Hector Berlioz to describe a recurring melody that is used obsessively. Berlioz first used the term in 1830 to describe the melody that represents the beloved in his *Symphonie Fantastique* and recurs in altered guises through each of the work's five movements, most famously in a grotesque, high-pitched, distorted version for E flat Clarinet in the final "Witches' Sabbath' movement. The term also has medical connotations and was associated by Balzac with clinical and criminal obsession.

impresario A manager of an opera season. The system of having impresarios run seasons began in Venice in the early seventeenth century with the emergence of the first public opera houses, owned by rich nobles who did not want the responsibility of running them. The practice then spread to other parts of Italy, and many parts of Europe.

leitmotif (German: "leading motif") Term coined by music historian A. W. Ambros in the mid-1860s to describe recurring themes or motifs, usually found in opera, which represent characters, objects, and emotions. Leitmotifs are particularly associated with Wagner's music dramas, which employ a complex web of leitmotifs.

Lied (plural Lieder) German art song typically associated with composers from the nineteenth century, particularly Schubert, Schumann, and Wolf. Lieder are generally written for solo voice and piano accompaniment. The accompaniments are often highly expressive and equal partners to the voice. Orchesterlieder are a variety of art song in which soloists are accompanied by the full orchestra rather than piano.

orchestration The art of scoring a piece of music, namely deciding which instruments or combinations of instruments should be assigned each part. Many composers begin by working out their ideas on the piano and developing the orchestration at a later stage. Medieval and Renaissance music often did not supply orchestration details, leaving decisions up to performers, partly depending on which instruments were available. Orchestration became particularly developed in the nineteenth century when new instruments became available, and composers such as Berlioz and Debussy paid particular attention to creating new sounds, experimenting with expressive combinations of instruments.

recitative (Italian: "recitational") A speech-like type of singing commonly found in opera and oratorio and invented around 1600 to make music subservient to the text. In contrast to the melodic "aria," recitative uses free rhythms (or rhythms derived from speech), and avoids structured, memorable melodies. Recitative could be accompanied by the orchestra (*recitativo accompagnato*) or continuo instruments, such as the keyboard and a bass instrument (*recitativo secco*). It is often used to convey dialog and narration, helping to move the action along, whereas arias are more static, giving characters an opportunity to reflect on their situation.

Romanticism A term used in the nineteenth century to describe a new spirit in art, politics, and philosophy. Romanticism embraced many competing interests, including a new emphasis on emotion and subjectivity over order, the interrelationships between the arts, nostalgia for nature and the past, a closer interest in national identity, and a fascination for the new and unusual, including the exotic and the supernatural.

salonnières Female hostesses of salons, which became particularly popular in France in the eighteenth and nineteenth centuries (though they have an even longer history). These women invited a select group of people to their salons to discuss artistic, philosophical, and political topics. Salonnières were well connected and highly influential, often providing financial support to their talented protégés, influencing fashions, and playing important roles in cultural institutions.

strophic form A term associated with vocal music in which each stanza is set to the same, or very similar, music. Hymns and folk songs are usually strophic. Schubert also used strophic form in some of his Lieder.

through-composed A composition that does not use repeated sections. The term is usually associated with songs in which each stanza of the text is set to different music.

timbre The quality or character of the sound of a particular instrument or voice or combination of instruments and/or voices.

LIEDER & SONG CYCLES

3-SECOND NOTE
The German term Lieder simply means "songs," but also "poems intended for singing," underlining the intimate relationship between lyrical poetry and its musical rendition.

3-MINUTE REFRAIN
Lieder often don't come singly, and the term "Song Cycle" entered the lexicography in Koch's *Musikalisches Lexikon* in 1865 to describe a group of individually complete songs designed to increase the scope of a genre that was often (falsely) considered second rate. Coherence was achieved through textual and/or musical procedures. During the course of the nineteenth century, the recapitulation of certain musical ideas throughout the cycle deepened the sense of cyclical conception.

Eighteenth-century Lieder feature a simple, usually strophic setting of German lyrical poems with mostly unremarkable melodies, conventional harmonies, and stock accompaniment figuration; the music was considered subsidiary to the poetry. A century on, the style became more sophisticated, developing into Kunstlied ("art song"), a distinct genre initially performed by educated amateur musicians—frequently females. A crucial characteristic of the genre was still a certain intimacy, the designated performance venue being the middle-class drawing room. However, music in nineteenth-century Lieder soon sought to express the literal imagery and emotional content of the text, making the composer equal to the poet in determining their emotional effect, and achieving not only a balance but a quintessentially Romantic synthesis of words and music. This innovative approach was pioneered by Schubert with his 1814 setting of "Gretchen am Spinnrade" (Gretchen at the Spinning Wheel), where the piano figuration expresses the wheel's motion and the protagonist's inner agitation. Lieder soon conquered the concert hall as well as the parlor through Liszt's piano transcriptions, while the genre was further developed through Orchesterlieder (for solo voice(s) and orchestra), which, in the late 1800s, became increasingly fashionable, the most prominent exponents being Liszt, Mahler, and Richard Strauss.

RELATED TOPICS
See also
FELIX MENDELSSOHN
page 92

SALON CULTURE
page 94

FRANZ LISZT
page 100

3-SECOND BIOGRAPHIES
FRANZ SCHUBERT
1797–1828
Austrian composer whose output of about 600 Lieder—arguably his most significant contribution to classical music—was complemented by eight symphonies, chamber and piano music, sacred and incidental music, and operas

ROBERT SCHUMANN
1810–56
German composer best known for his cyclical approach to characteristic piano pieces, his profusion of Lieder and song cycles, symphonies, and chamber works

EXPERT
Monika Hennemann

Lieder often celebrate the beauty of the German landscape.

1925
Born in Berlin

1943
Drafted into the
German army

1945
Taken prisoner by the
British army

1947
Concert debut in
Freiburg, as the baritone
soloist for Brahms' *Ein
deutsches Requiem*

1954–56
Performs at the Bayreuth
Festival in *Lohengrin*,
Tannhäuser, *Parsifal*,
and *Die Meistersinger
von Nürnberg*

1951
British debut, in Delius'
A Mass of Life; first
performs with pianist
Gerald Moore

1962
Soloist in the premiere of
Britten's *War Requiem*,
Coventry Cathedral

1970–71
Records the complete
Schubert Lieder with
Moore for Deutsche
Grammophon

1971
Publishes *Auf den Spuren
der Schubert-Lieder:
Werden, Wesen, Wirkung*
(subsequently translated
as *Schubert's Songs: A
Biographical Study*)

1973
First recording as a
conductor, of Schubert's
Fifth and Eighth
Symphonies, with the
New Philharmonic
Orchestra, London

1980
First exhibition of his
artworks in Bamberg

1992
Gives his final
performance, at the
National Theatre in
Munich

2012
Dies in Bavaria

DIETRICH FISCHER-DIESKAU

One of the greatest singers of the twentieth century, Fischer-Dieskau is now primarily remembered for his huge contribution to recording and performing German Lieder.

His early studies were interrupted by military service in the 1940s, and he did not give his first solo recital until 1948. Over the course of the next decade, he became highly sought after as an operatic singer—in works by Wagner, Richard Strauss, Mozart, and Verdi—and performed at leading venues and events such as the Vienna Staatsoper, La Scala, and the Bayreuth and Salzburg Festivals. He also worked with many contemporary composers, creating roles in operas by Hans Werner Henze and Aribert Reimann, and performing solos in new choral works by composers Benjamin Britten, Michael Tippett, Igor Stravinsky, and Witold Lutosławski.

Fischer-Dieskau began his famed partnership with the British pianist Gerald Moore in 1951, the same year in which he first performed in Britain. This was a crucial pairing, not only for its musical acumen, but also for the rehabilitation of German song (and German performers) in the UK after the Second World War. He and Moore performed countless times together, commanding a huge repertoire of Lieder (more than 1,000 songs in all), and recording all the songs of Schubert, Schumann, Brahms, Wolf, and Strauss suitable for a male singer.

With Moore and other pianists, including Daniel Barenboim and Jörg Demus, he also recorded the majority of Lieder composed by Mendelssohn, Beethoven, Berg, and Haydn, as well as other repertoire by Liszt, Debussy, Strauss, Schoenberg, and Hindemith. He was an inventive concert programmer, and earned tremendous critical acclaim for the clarity of his diction, refined and flawless vocal technique, and for his subtle employment of color and nuance in the delivery of both words and music.

This interest in performing and recording Lieder was matched by Fischer-Dieskau's intellectual curiosity: He published books on the vocal music of Schumann, Schubert, and Wolf, as well as texts about Wagner and Nietzsche, Debussy, and Eduard Mörike. In 1976, he issued *The Fischer-Dieskau Book of Lieder*, a collection of well-known song texts and their translations. He held teaching positions at the Akademie der Künste and the Musikhochschule in Berlin, and published his memoirs, *Nachklang* (Echoes) in 1988.

From 1973, Fischer-Dieskau began to appear as a conductor, working with orchestras in England and Germany. From 1980, he also began to exhibit his paintings. He continued to sing in concert and operatic performances until 1992.

Katy Hamilton

FELIX MENDELSSOHN

RELATED TOPICS
See also
ORATORIO
page 60

THE SYMPHONY
page 76

SALON CULTURE
page 94

PROGRAM MUSIC
page 98

3-SECOND NOTE

Felix Mendelssohn was a major player in early nineteenth-century European musical life, achieving fame as a composer, conductor, performer, and founder of the Leipzig Conservatory.

3-MINUTE REFRAIN

Mendelssohn was a Lutheran German of Jewish ancestry, and his output admittedly oscillates between genuinely great works and elegant salon pieces of modest musical merits. Nevertheless, the reputation of even his finest pieces was tarnished for decades by anti-Semitic criticisms by Wagner and his followers, and by the bourgeois Victorian sentimentality allegedly displayed by much of his music. In recent decades, however, his historical importance and innovative genius has been more fully recognized.

Perhaps the single most remarkable child prodigy in the history of Western music, Mendelssohn (1809–47) was a master of illustrative music, and a Romantic composer constantly drawn to the older classical forms, which he nevertheless treated in a new and subtle manner. His fascination with the music of his great German predecessors such as Bach, Handel, and Schubert also prompted him to promote early music both as an editor, and as conductor of several series of "historical concerts" with the renowned Leipzig Gewandhaus Orchestra. He contributed to all the major musical genres of his time, and even established some of his own—the "concert overture," a self-standing, programmatic orchestral work, such as the *Hebrides* overture; and the *Songs without Words*—pleasing solo piano pieces for cultivated and moderately ambitious amateur performers, of which the "Spring Song" is the best known. Many of his most famous compositions were, astonishingly, completed in his late teens, including the remarkable String Octet (1825) and *Midsummer Night's Dream* overture (1826). Other masterpieces include his Symphony No. 3 "*Scottish*," the oratorio *Elijah*, and the Violin Concerto in E Minor. During his lifetime, he was also influential as pianist, music educator, and unofficial cultural ambassador for German Romanticism in Europe.

3-SECOND BIOGRAPHIES

CARL FRIEDRICH ZELTER
1758–1832
German musical autodidact, founder and director of the Berlin Singakademie; he taught composition to Mendelssohn, Fanny Hensel, Giacomo Meyerbeer, and Otto Nicolai

JENNY LIND
1820–87
Swedish soprano and a friend of Mendelssohn, who tailored music specifically for her voice

EXPERT
Monika Hennemann

Mendelssohn was rumored to be romantically interested in Swedish soprano Jenny Lind.

SALON CULTURE

Salons were usually hosted by political or cultural figures, such as Princess Mathilde Bonaparte, Dorothea Schlegel, and Sara Levy. A major part of a musician's career (and earnings) could be derived from salon performances and compositions, since well-connected salonnières sought to present noted artists as a mark of their own cultural sophistication—this could lead to commissions, further performance opportunities, and teaching work. The salon was a particularly important space for women, who were seldom able to publish compositions or perform with the public freedom of male counterparts. Noted female composers during the 1800s include Luise Reichardt, Josephine Lang, and Fanny Mendelssohn, who wrote songs, piano works, and chamber pieces for their invited audiences. It was also thanks to the power of the salon that Chopin, who did not enjoy performing in large-scale public concerts, was able to disseminate his works and acquire influential admirers and pupils. Compositions written for salon performance had to be fashionable and charming, and included dance music, songs, and arrangements of well-known operatic melodies. Some—such as the works of Chopin, Chabrier, and Elgar—combined style with musical sophistication; but many "pot-boilers" were simply produced to amuse audiences.

3-SECOND NOTE
The salon was a private space, opened to an invited public for the exchange and enjoyment of culture and conversation: literary readings, music-making, and philosophical debate.

3-MINUTE REFRAIN
The questionable artistic worth of much salon music led to scathing critical attacks even at the time, with some writers attempting to differentiate between good, "noble" amateur music-making, and the vapid and superficial effects of late-nineteenth-century salon writing. However, the salon continued to hold sway as an important cultural space until at least the 1940s, and provided valuable opportunities for artists to try out and discuss new ideas.

RELATED TOPICS
See also
CHAMBER MUSIC
page 74

FELIX MENDELSSOHN
page 92

3-SECOND BIOGRAPHIES
LUISE REICHARDT
1779–1826
German composer, daughter of composer Johann Friedrich Reichardt; she knew many leading literary figures of the day through her father's salon

FANNY MENDELSSOHN
1805–47
German pianist, composer, and Mendelssohn's elder sister; she hosted a highly regarded salon in Berlin, where many of her own works were performed

FRYDERYK CHOPIN
1810–49
Polish pianist, composer, and noted exponent of short dance pieces, suitable for salons

EXPERT
Katy Hamilton

Josephine Lang (1815–80) was a singer, teacher, and composer, whose Lieder were praised by Mendelssohn.

PARTING SONG

FOR AN ALTO VOICE

WITH

Pianoforte

JOSEPHINE LANG

HECTOR BERLIOZ

3-SECOND NOTE
Imaginative, intensely emotional, and obsessive in love, Berlioz is the quintessential romantic artist whose music often reflected his turbulent emotional life.

3-MINUTE REFRAIN
Berlioz complained bitterly about his necessary and lucrative work as a music critic because it diverted him from composition. He was an accomplished writer: witty, perceptive, and informative about the musical practices of his day. His treatise *Grand traité d'instrumentation et d'orchestration modernes* draws examples from composers he admired, particularly Gluck. The work is a testament to Berlioz' mastery of expressive orchestration; his compositions exploited the new timbres of the period's expanding romantic orchestra.

Known for his highly dramatic music, Hector Berlioz (1803–69) composed works focusing on key themes of romanticism: forbidden love and death in *Roméo et Juliette*, melancholy and isolation in *Harold en Italie,* and unrequited love in the semi-autobiographical *Symphonie Fantastique*, which traces an artist's opium-induced dreams about his beloved. The "beloved," represented through a recurring melody (or idée fixe), was the Shakespearian actress, Harriet Smithson, whom Berlioz later married. Paris was Berlioz's home, but he struggled to secure performances of his music in the city. His ambitions focused on the Paris Opéra. Berlioz completed five operas, of which *Les Troyens* is his masterpiece. Taking Virgil's *Aeneid* as its subject, it is epic in proportion. Berlioz breathes passion into his characters and creates contrasting moods with his expressive orchestration. The opera was performed in a heavily cut form in Berlioz's lifetime with some success, but the composer did not approve of the liberties taken with his score. Today, Berlioz is mostly known as a symphonist. Even so, his operatic impulses are always evident; his orchestral writing suggests voices, actions, and gestures, and incorporates theatrical devices, such as off-stage music. He even employs choruses and recitative in *Roméo et Juliette*.

RELATED TOPICS
See also
THE SYMPHONY
page 76

PROGRAM MUSIC
page 98

FRANZ LISZT
page 100

THE ORCHESTRA
page 106

3-SECOND BIOGRAPHIES
CHRISTOPH WILLIBALD GLUCK
1714–87
Bohemian composer who instigated operatic reforms that advocated composers' greater attention to the dramatic meaning of the text

LUIGI CHERUBINI
1760–1842
Italian opera composer who, as director of the Paris Conservatoire, was frequently at loggerheads with Berlioz

EXPERT
Joanne Cormac

Berlioz was profoundly moved by Harriet Smithson's performances of Ophelia and Juliet in Paris in 1827.

PROGRAM MUSIC

The term "program" music has been understood in a number of different ways. It can refer to imitative music that attempts to depict an object. More often, however, it is understood as representing a non-musical subject (say a painting or poem) in an indirect way, or as generating the same mood in listeners that they would experience when contemplating the subject itself. Composers have long attempted to depict non-musical imagery, particularly nature, as in Vivaldi's *The Four Seasons*. However, the term was only introduced in the nineteenth century by Liszt. This coincided with a new interest in interrelationships between the arts. The concept also developed out of a need to address the future of music after Beethoven, whose output, for many composers, represented a height that seemed impossible to surpass. Advocates of program music felt that Beethoven revealed the way forward with "programmatic" works, such as the *Pastoral Symphony*. Most program music is composed for solo piano or orchestra. Prominent examples include the symphonic poems of Liszt, Smetana, and Dvořák, Berlioz's dramatic symphonies, and the tone poems of Strauss, Tchaikovsky, and the Mighty Handful. Typically, such works are presented with an evocative title or a printed preface, explaining the meaning behind the piece.

3-SECOND NOTE
Many composers, listeners, and philosophers have expressed skepticism that music can represent a non-musical subject, but program music claims to do just that.

3-MINUTE REFRAIN
By the mid-nineteenth century many composers had lost faith in the idea of program music and began to propose an ideal of pure, autonomous, instrumental music, which did not seek to represent extra-musical meaning. It became known as "absolute music." Its advocates felt that making music depict an extra-musical subject subverted the essential nature of music, and a bitter feud ensued in the press between representatives of the two schools of thought.

RELATED TOPICS
See also
LUDWIG VAN BEETHOVEN
page 78

HECTOR BERLIOZ
page 96

FRANZ LISZT
page 100

THE MIGHTY HANDFUL
page 118

3-SECOND BIOGRAPHIES
FRANZ BRENDEL
1811–68
German writer, lecturer, and editor of the periodical *Die Neue Zeitschrift für Musik*, a key organ for promoting program music

EDUARD HANSLICK
1825–1904
German music critic, aesthetician, and author of an influential treatise, *On the Musically Beautiful*, criticizing the concept of program music

EXPERT
Joanne Cormac

Program music was inspired by painting, sculpture, poetry, drama, and mythology.

FRANZ LISZT

Captivating, charismatic, and a formidably talented pianist, Liszt (1811–86) was one of the most famous musicians of his day and enjoyed a highly successful career as a touring virtuoso. He was a pioneer, developing new playing techniques and creating the solo recital (before Liszt, variety concerts including multiple performers were the norm). In 1848, Liszt retired from concert touring to become conductor of the Weimar Court Theatre, a decision that provoked surprise (Weimar was a small town for such a big personality), but he wanted to concentrate on composition. In Weimar, Liszt also developed conducting techniques, promoted new works by Berlioz, Wagner, and Schumann, and developed a new orchestral genre: the symphonic poem. The symphonic poems depicted "extramusical" ideas, such as mythological figures or works of art. Liszt completed 13 symphonic poems on subjects including Hamlet, Orpheus, and Prometheus. In Weimar, Liszt also completed one of his most formally innovative works, the B Minor Sonata. Born in Hungary, Liszt was also a figurehead for Hungarian nationalism and composed many works inspired by Hungarian themes, including the *Hungarian Rhapsodies*. The austerity and radical harmonic experiments of his late piano works, including *Nuages Gris*, anticipated the dissonances of modern music.

3-SECOND NOTE
Liszt is best known as the greatest pianist of his time, provoking hysteria in audiences, but his wide-ranging impact on music history is often overlooked.

3-MINUTE REFRAIN
Liszt's music has often been criticized for being showy and excessive. However, even works designed to please a crowd, such as his numerous opera transcriptions, were often stunningly original. His experiments with form, harmony, thematic transformation, and new piano techniques and textures had an important influence on other composers, including Wagner, Richard Strauss, and Debussy. Liszt's enormous impact on music history encompassed a broad variety of fields, including performance practices, conducting, teaching, and composition.

3-SECOND BIOGRAPHIES
GAËTANO BELLONI
1810–87
Italian manager of Liszt's concert tours from 1841–47

PRINCESS CAROLYNE VON SAYN WITTGENSTEIN
1819–87
Polish aristocrat and Liszt's partner from the late 1840s; their planned wedding was thwarted in 1861 when the annulment of Carolyne's previous marriage was refused

EXPERT
Joanne Cormac

Josef Danhauser's painting of Liszt at the piano surrounded by admirers and watched over by Beethoven, helped to cultivate Liszt's public image.

VIRTUOSITY

In its most basic sense, virtuosity is simply the possession of great technical skill in musical performance, and hence a valuable asset. Nevertheless, some critics see virtuosity as a potentially negative quality, arguing that "virtuosi" (musicians with notable virtuosity) often draw excessive attention to their purely technical skills—overshadowing the emotional meaning of the music, and producing superficially brilliant but shallow, posturing performances. Such criticisms have been voiced from at least the time of Plato. They find echoes in Mozart's condemnation of his rival Clementi as a "mere technician," in Wagner's and Mendelssohn's disparagement of the "party tricks" of contemporary nineteenth-century virtuosi, and in more recent criticisms of pianists such as Cziffra and Horowitz. Yet the two most celebrated virtuosi in history—Paganini on the violin, and Liszt on the piano—were far more than tastelessly talented showmen. Even Mendelssohn admitted that Liszt was a "true virtuoso," uniting exceptional technical skill with profound emotional understanding, and all successful performers must possess enough virtuosity to communicate convincingly with their audiences. The battle over the value of virtuosity is ultimately an argument over musical taste, namely whether the taste of the virtuoso happens to chime with that of the critic concerned.

RELATED TOPICS
See also
THE PIANO
page 82

FRANZ LISZT
page 100

3-SECOND BIOGRAPHIES
NICOLÒ PAGANINI
1782–1840
Italian virtuoso who laid the technical foundation of most later Romantic violin playing

FERRUCCIO BUSONI
1866–1924
Italian virtuoso, one of the most influential pianists after Liszt and Anton Rubinstein; his visionary compositions further expanded the technical possibilities of the instrument

VLADIMIR HOROWITZ
1903–89
Probably the most successful and contentious pianist of the late twentieth century

EXPERT
Kenneth Hamilton

Mozart and Clementi were two rivals in one of the world's first keyboard competitions.

RICHARD WAGNER

German composer Richard Wagner (1813–83) is traditionally seen as the enemy of brevity. He composed vast operas—his four-part *Der Ring des Nibelungen* requires four long evenings, and *Parsifal* lasts as long as all nine Beethoven symphonies—and he led a life of extraordinary incident. Composing almost exclusively for the operatic stage, he revolutionized that artform and, arguably, music as a whole: *Tristan und Isolde* all but ignored the rules of conventional harmony. This and other works, often heard as orchestral excerpts performed in concert, fused psychology, philosophy, and—despite mythological settings—profoundly human drama, and proved enormously influential on composers, writers, and visual artists. Wagner's musical freedom was partly due to his being guided only by the texts (which he wrote himself) rather than the prevalent instrumental forms. Indeed, one of his theories was that the purely instrumental symphony was a spent force, as Beethoven's use of singers in his Ninth had demonstrated. Wagner nevertheless adopted symphonic techniques, tying the vast "through-composed" acts of his operas together with a complex system of "leitmotifs." The rich orchestration, harmonic adventurousness, and soaring interweaving melodies of his music, against which singers often struggle to be heard, are difficult to resist—though many have tried.

3-SECOND NOTE
Hugely influential—as well as controversial—far beyond the world of classical music, Wagner was a towering genius of nineteenth-century music.

3-MINUTE REFRAIN
Much of Wagner's controversial status derives from his anti-Semitism, and debate continues to rage as to the extent that the man can be separated from the work, and to what extent Wagner's political beliefs should color our interpretation of his works. The question is made more complex and contentious by the fact that, 50 years after his death, Wagner was pushed into the service of Hitler's Third Reich. His music remains unofficially banned in Israel to this day.

RELATED TOPICS
See also
HECTOR BERLIOZ
page 96

FRANZ LISZT
page 100

THE CONCERT HALL
page 120

3-SECOND BIOGRAPHIES
COSIMA WAGNER
1837–1930
Daughter of Franz Liszt and Wagner's second wife; they married in 1870, and she retained an iron grip over the Bayreuth Festival for nearly half a century after his death

KING LUDWIG II
1845–86
"Mad" King Ludwig of Bavaria who was a passionate Wagner lover and, on ascending the throne, began to bankroll performances of his works, not to mention his lavish lifestyle

EXPERT
Hugo Shirley

Wagner built his own opera house in Bayreuth, Germany, founding a festival that runs to this day.

THE ORCHESTRA

RELATED TOPICS
See also
THE SYMPHONY
page 76

THE CONDUCTOR
page 114

THE CONCERT HALL
page 120

THE SCORE
page 124

3-SECOND NOTE
The bedrock of so much classical music, the symphony orchestra and its home, the concert hall, today are monuments of civic pride.

3-MINUTE REFRAIN
A modern symphony orchestra employs dozens of highly trained musicians who must be equally adept at quickly learning new music and adapting to different interpretations of familiar music, taking the limelight in purely orchestral works, sharing it with soloists and choruses in concertos and oratorios, or being confined to the pit in an opera house. The size of the modern orchestra demands a great deal of discipline from the musicians, with the role of the conductor—and an accurate score and orchestral parts—becoming especially important.

Groups of musicians have accompanied various events—social and theatrical—for centuries if not millennia, and indeed the word orchestra derives from a Latin word describing the area occupied in front of a stage by musicians. Nevertheless, the modern idea of the orchestra in classical music, of a regulated and regular group of musicians playing a prescribed array of instruments, originated in late seventeenth-century Paris, becoming increasingly standardized across Europe during the early years of the eighteenth century. Defined simply, the orchestra consists of a corpus of stringed instruments, with multiple musicians to each part, variously bolstered by wind, brass, and percussion instruments. The standard orchestra of the classical period grew—both in size and variety—up to the beginning of the twentieth century, with composers often tailoring their music to the strengths or special resources likely to be at their disposal. The nineteenth century saw orchestras increasingly coming under control of civic bodies and impresarios rather than courts, taking on a conductor as figurehead. Today, traditional "symphony" orchestras playing on modern instruments are also complemented by groups that set out, often on period instruments, to recreate earlier forms of the orchestra.

3-SECOND BIOGRAPHIES
BERLIN PHILHARMONIC ORCHESTRA
founded 1882
Often considered to be the world's finest orchestra, the Berlin Philharmonic attracts many musicians who have enjoyed careers as soloists

ACADEMY OF ANCIENT MUSIC
founded 1973
Cambridge-based period instrument orchestra, founded by Christopher Hogwood

EXPERT
Hugo Shirley

Bringing together all major instruments, the orchestra is the bedrock of great classical music.

THE LATE NINETEENTH &
EARLY TWENTIETH CENTURIES

THE LATE NINETEENTH & EARLY TWENTIETH CENTURIES
GLOSSARY

absolute music In contrast to program music, absolute music is not intended to represent an extra-musical subject, say a poem or painting or even an emotion. Instead, it is considered to be abstract and autonomous. Absolute music contains no words, as a text would lend a representational quality to the music, so the term usually refers to instrumental rather than vocal music.

articulation While dynamics tell performers how loudly to produce a sound, articulation instructs performers about the intended character of that sound. A common articulation instruction is *staccato* (Italian: "detached"). The opposite of staccato is "legato," meaning that the music should be played smoothly. Articulation is notated in various ways. Dots, small wedges, and vertical lines above the notes are used to indicate staccato, whereas a curved line above a group of notes indicates that they should be played smoothly, without noticeable breaks between each note.

dissonance Two or more notes played together that produce a discord, which is jarring to the ear. Playing adjacent notes in the scale will produce a dissonance. Traditionally, in classical music dissonances are "resolved" with a consonant chord, which sounds harmonious, stable, and complete. However, dissonance has often been used for expressive reasons, in order to aid expression of madrigal texts. In the nineteenth century composers experimented further with dissonance, introducing new harmonies, and avoiding or prolonging the time until resolution. Many twentieth-century composers were influenced by Schoenberg's idea of the "emancipation of the dissonance," treating traditionally dissonant chords as stable harmonies.

figuration A term often used to describe passagework or accompaniment with an easily identifiable, repeated shape, e.g. an arpeggio.

fugue (Italian *fuga*: "flight") A compositional technique. In the first section, or "exposition," a short melodic line, or "subject," is imitated in successive voices (described thus whether they are instrumental or vocal). When the subject has been heard in all voices a new section (an "episode") begins, developing material that has occurred in the exposition and usually modulating to a new key. Then the subject returns and the rest of the piece consists of alternations between subject entries and episodes.

maestro A title given in Italy to celebrated composers, performers, conductors, and music teachers.

mode An early type of scale devised to classify chants to make them easier to learn and remember. Originally, the eight church modes were simply given numbers, but in the ninth century some writers applied the names of Greek scales (e.g. dorian and mixolydian) to the church modes. Modern Western modes use some of the same Greek names, but they are quite different from medieval church modes. Modern modes offer an alternative to the traditional major scale as the makeup of intervals is different. They are often found in folk and jazz music, and many composers, such as Debussy and Bartók, have used modes to extend the possibilities of traditional harmony and introduce new and unusual sounds that have an archaic or exotic flavor.

passacaglia form In the early seventeenth century a passacaglia was a repeated interlude (or ritornello) played before or between the verses of a song. However, it soon evolved into a new form, developed by Frescobaldi in the late 1620s. In this guise the passacaglia comprised variations of a melody played over a repeated bassline, known as a "ground bass."

phrasing Pieces of music often fall naturally into phrases (shorter sections of music). A short melody might consist of one phrase; a longer one might consist of two—one that seems equivalent to a question and one that acts as an answer. In some ways phrasing is similar to punctuation, indicating short breaks between lines of music. Often, it is instinctual; good phrasing allows performers to make sense of the music, rather than understanding it as one undifferentiated sound.

pitch A term referring to where a note falls within a scale, whether high or low. Variations of pitch depend on the speed at which the sound is vibrating. Fast vibrations produce a high pitch and slow vibrations a low one.

repertory A collection of works that a performer or institution has ready for a performance. "Standard repertory" usually refers to the works performed most often.

staff (plural staves) A series of five horizontal lines used to notate certain pitches. Composers place notes on or between the lines in order to indicate the particular note intended and its relationship to other notes.

texture Denotes the relationship of the parts within a piece of music to one another. A single part sounding alone is a monophonic texture, a melody and harmony is a homophonic texture and several independent voices sounding simultaneously is a polyphonic texture.

tonality The key in which a piece of music is written or played—such as C major. Tonal music has a recognizable key, atonal music does not.

NATIONALISM

3-SECOND NOTE
Nationalist music emerged in the nineteenth century alongside political independence movements, and also became a means of reaction against the dominance of the Austro-German-dominated classical tradition.

3-MINUTE REFRAIN
Nationalism has been a source of inspiration for many composers, but people disagree about whether music can actually express nationalist content. Sometimes music seems to contain stylistic features that are associated with a particular national identity, but some nationalist music—such as Wagner's—does not. Instead, nationalism in music has often been seen as a product of the context in which it is composed and the way it is received.

Revolutions and political upheaval of the late eighteenth and nineteenth centuries meant that Europe's map was constantly redrawn as people fought for freedom and democracy, for their country's independence from a larger power, or for its unification. This created a potent situation in which nationalist movements could thrive. These movements inspired a collective sense of identity by emphasizing a community's shared language, land, and cultural heritage. Music has long been a powerful indicator of national identity, playing an important role in nationalist projects. Some composers have actively sought to compose nationalist music, drawing on national folksongs and tales (deemed to embody the "authentic" character of a community), promoting the national language, and developing a style that captures the feeling of the nation. For example, *Kullervo*, a suite for orchestra and chorus by Sibelius, is based on texts compiled from Finnish myths and folklore. It combines "authentic" texts and idiomatic setting of the Finnish language with recognizably "Finnish" music, characterized by its use of modally tinged melodies, obsessive repetition, and thick, dark, minor-mode textures, seemingly redolent of Finland's tragic history. Similarly, Smetana's symphonic poem *Má Vlast* depicts aspects of the Bohemian countryside and history.

RELATED TOPICS
See also
RICHARD WAGNER
page 104

THE MIGHTY HANDFUL
page 118

AARON COPLAND
page 140

3-SECOND BIOGRAPHIES
JACOB & WILHELM GRIMM
1785–1863 & 1786–1859
German academics best known for their collection of German folktales, used during the Third Reich to foster nationalism

BEDŘICH SMETANA
1824–84
Czech composer

JEAN SIBELIUS
1865–1957
Finnish composer

EXPERT
Joanne Cormac

A national hero in Finland, Sibelius created a distinctly Finnish sound, primarily in his orchestral music.

THE CONDUCTOR

3-SECOND NOTE
The conductor's role grew out of modest and entirely practical beginnings to take on talismanic importance in performances involving multiple musicians.

3-MINUTE REFRAIN
For various historical reasons, conductors were generally male until the later years of the twentieth century, with both masculinity as well as a certain brand of musical authoritarianism often seen as essential characteristics of a "maestro." In recent decades, however, efforts have been made to address the gender imbalance within the profession.

A reasonable question for anyone attending a classical symphonic concert for the first time might be: What does that person waving their arms around at the front do? The answer is complex. The conductor not only galvanizes a performance in the moment, usually beating time with one hand (either with or without a baton) and highlighting expression with the other, but also leads rehearsals, in which technical and interpretative aspects are decided upon: speeds, tempo fluctuations, and the balancing of the instruments. The practical side of the role has a long history, and is related to that of singers who marked the units of time in early polyphony, and musicians who, in the seventeenth and eighteenth centuries, led performances from the keyboard or violin. The conductor's role as we know it, however, was developed in the nineteenth century and was in part a reaction to the challenges posed by the increasingly complex works being composed. It also reflected the need for an interpretive figurehead imbued with sufficient authority to preside over performances of those pieces that were at the time starting to form the canon: a repertory of Great Works by composers of acknowledged genius. Today's conductors continue to play that role, while increasingly serving as figureheads of the orchestras and institutions they direct.

RELATED TOPICS
See also
FELIX MENDELSSOHN
page 92

HECTOR BERLIOZ
page 96

THE ORCHESTRA
page 106

LEONARD BERNSTEIN
page 116

3-SECOND BIOGRAPHIES
GUSTAV MAHLER
1860–1911
Austrian composer, famous in his lifetime as the controversial and talismanic conductor of the Vienna Court Opera and Philharmonic Orchestra

MARIN ALSOP
1956–
American conductor who became the first woman to conduct the BBC's Last Night of the Proms in 2013

EXPERT
Hugo Shirley

The conductor guides the orchestra in interpretation as much as technical execution.

1918
Born in Lawrence, Massachusetts

1940
Attends the Tanglewood summer school, where he studies with Koussevitzky

1943
His unscheduled appearance with the New York Philharmonic brings him national attention

1944
His musical *On the Town* is a hit

1957
West Side Story opens on Broadway; a movie version follows in 1961

1958
Becomes music director of the New York Philharmonic: following a decade in post, he is appointed Laureate Conductor for Life

1966
Viennese debut conducting Beethoven's *Fidelio* at the State Opera

1971
Written in memory of John F. Kennedy, his *Mass* is given an equivocal reception in Washington

1976
His final musical, *1600 Pennsylvania Avenue*, flops badly

1983
A Quiet Place, his only full-length opera, debuts disastrously in Houston

1990
Dies in New York

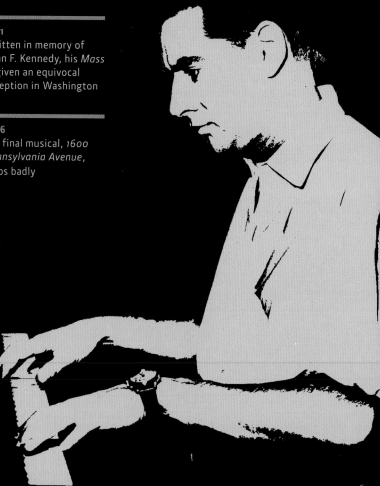

LEONARD BERNSTEIN

In an era when conductors reached the height of fame and glamor, Leonard Bernstein was one of the most famous and certainly the most glamorous; but he was a multifaceted musician—a pianist and an educator as well as a successful composer.

Born in 1918 in Lawrence, Massachusetts, to a family of Russian-Jewish immigrants, Bernstein was drawn to music from an early age. He studied at Harvard and took piano lessons, also informally studying conducting with Dimitri Mitropoulos; he went on to the Curtis Institute in Philadelphia and further conducting lessons with Serge Koussevitzky.

In 1943, he was offered the assistant conductorship of the New York Philharmonic; his national breakthrough came in November of that year when at short notice he took over a broadcast concert due to be led by Bruno Walter.

Meanwhile, he had started to make his name as a composer, with such serious works as his *Jeremiah Symphony*, premiered in January 1944, a few months before the ballet *Fancy Free*, which later that same year formed the narrative basis of his musical *On the Town*. Switching between serious and popular genres would become a hallmark of his career, which reached its peak with *West Side Story* in 1957.

As a conductor, Bernstein worked internationally, commencing a long-term relationship with the Israel Philharmonic in 1948, another with La Scala in Milan from 1953, and a crucial relationship in Vienna, where he gained a loyal following for his work with the Philharmonic as well as for his work with the State Opera on his debut in 1966. For a decade from 1959, he was the music director of the New York Philharmonic.

Though out of sympathy with avant-garde trends, Bernstein conducted a good deal of contemporary music. An intensely emotional conductor, he had a deep rapport with Mahler, whose music he helped popularize. His platform manner was energetic to the point of showy, though even those who thought it crowd-pleasing could not fault the results. As an educator, his most notable initiative was the Young People's Concerts at the New York Philharmonic, whose broadcasts (1958–72) raised public interest in classical music in the United States to an unprecedented level.

As a composer, his lasting legacy lies in his works for the musical theater, especially *West Side Story*; his own style was eclectic, moving between punchy jazz-influenced scores and cooler "serious" concert works—although these never achieved the same level of approval as his musicals. The irony was that his busy conducting career kept him from his writing desk; just a week before his death in October 1990, he announced his retirement from conducting to concentrate on composition.

George Hall

THE MIGHTY HANDFUL

RELATED TOPIC
See also
NATIONALISM
page 112

3-SECOND NOTE
The *Moguchaya Kuchka* (Mighty Handful) was a group of five Russian composers who sought to develop a national musical style distinctive from that of Western Europe.

The members of the Mighty Handful were Mily Balakirev (1837–1910), Aleksandr Borodin (1833–87), César Cui (1835–1918), Modest Mussorgsky (1839–81), and Nikolay Rimsky-Korsakov (1844–1908). Balakirev acted as their leader, but the five only worked closely together from about 1860 to 1870. None of them received formal musical training. They were inspired by the ideas of the critic Vladimir Stasov (who also coined the group's nickname) and the works of Mikhail Glinka, who had sought to incorporate folk melodies into his compositions. Preexisting folksongs and dances, melodies based on Russian melodic structures, and even "Oriental" music feature in their work, reflecting the varied landscape of their vast country. Mussorgsky also wrote several operas based on Russian historical themes, including *Boris Godunov* and *Khovanshchina*, while Rimsky-Korsakov produced operatic settings of several of Nikolay Gogol's stories. A commitment to setting the Russian language was significant, since it was only with writers such as Pushkin, in the early nineteenth century, that it had been considered a language fit for literature and high art. Following Mussorgsky's early death, Rimsky-Korsakov did much to complete his unfinished works and ensure their publication.

3-SECOND BIOGRAPHIES
MIKHAIL GLINKA
1804–57
Russian composer, the first to incorporate folk material into his musical language, and to write operas on Russian national themes

ANTON RUBINSTEIN
1829–94
Russian concert pianist of international repute and the first director of the St. Petersburg Conservatory, founded in 1862, which brought him into conflict with the Mighty Handful

PYOTR IL'YICH TCHAIKOVSKY
1840–93
Russian composer whose symphonies, ballets, and operas blend Russian themes and models with a variety of European musical structures

3-MINUTE REFRAIN
At a time when Russian music was dominated by Western European models, the Mighty Handful wanted to find a compositional approach that more properly represented the music and culture of their country. They were scathing about the newly founded St. Petersburg State Conservatory, which promoted Western musical models. Tchaikovsky was among its first students, although several of his early works reflect an interest in folk models, which suggests that he was interested in both European approaches and the ideas of the nationalist group.

EXPERT
Katy Hamilton

Boris Godunov is set shortly after the construction of St. Basil's Cathedral (1561).

THE CONCERT HALL

3-SECOND NOTE

A public building, usually designed to provide a suitable acoustic space for the performance of live music, the concert hall at its most basic consists of a stage and an auditorium.

3-MINUTE REFRAIN

The internal and external features of concert halls can reveal much about the perception of the music being performed there. Nineteenth-century European halls often feature busts or name-plaques of composers, almost in the manner of a religious building (such as the Vienna Musikverein); while twentieth- and twenty-first-century halls privilege superior acoustics and facilities within visually striking architectural shapes (for example, the Walt Disney Concert Hall in Los Angeles).

Much music composed before the 1750s was written with very specific performance spaces in mind: churches, the court, theaters, or private chambers. In the later eighteenth century, public concerts began to emerge as an increasingly popular form of entertainment and they required suitable venues in which to accommodate musicians and their audiences. Many of the best-known concert spaces from the eighteenth and early nineteenth centuries were not intended for music at all: The Leipzig Gewandhaus was originally a drapers' hall; Vienna used its court buildings; and casinos were also a common venue type. As public concerts became more prevalent and cheaper to attend, they also came to affect compositional approaches: chamber music became grander and more rhetorical, orchestras and choirs larger, to suit newly-constructed buildings and growing audiences. Music was no longer the court's exclusive privilege but a public asset, and it demanded grand civic buildings—from London's Royal Albert Hall (1871) and Queen's Hall (1893) to the open-air Hollywood Bowl (1922) in California. From the mid-1800s, program notes helped to educate new audiences.

RELATED TOPICS

See also
JOSEPH HAYDN
page 72

THE ORCHESTRA
page 106

THE CONDUCTOR
page 114

3-SECOND BIOGRAPHIES

MARTIN GROPIUS
1824–80
German architect of the second Leipzig Gewandhaus (1884), which was the inspiration for Amsterdam's Concertgebouw and Symphony Hall, Boston

WILLIAM BURNET TUTHILL
1855–1929
American historian, acoustician, and architect who designed Carnegie Hall, New York, following his extensive study of European concert hall construction

EXPERT

Katy Hamilton

Seating plans provide insights into the layout of eighteenth- and nineteenth-century concert halls.

STAGE

JOHANNES BRAHMS

3-SECOND NOTE
Brahms was one of the most important composers of "absolute" instrumental music, songs, and choral pieces in the second half of the nineteenth century.

3-MINUTE REFRAIN
Brahms was very conscious of his place in history, as a would-be successor to Beethoven, and a performer and conductor with an interest in earlier music. He was a skilled editor, producing editions of works by Couperin, Mozart, Chopin, Schubert, and Schumann. As a result, he became aware of what posterity might make of his own paper trail. So he disposed of as many sketches, rejected pieces, and letters as he could, trying to preserve his posthumous privacy.

Robert Schumann feted Johannes Brahms (1833–97) as the composer who would provide the next great innovations in traditional musical forms—sonatas and symphonies above all—championed by Beethoven. A keen student of early music, including Bach, Handel, and Schütz, Brahms sought to enrich his instrumental and choral writing by using devices from Baroque and Renaissance compositions, including passacaglia form (in the Fourth Symphony), fugue, and canon. His determination to breathe new life into Classical genres placed him in opposition to Liszt and Wagner, who wanted to create new forms for a new age. Brahms was also interested in folksong, collecting melodies, and composing new music in folk style. His compositions range from the highly virtuosic and musically complex, such as the Violin Concerto, *Ein deutsches Requiem,* and the late piano pieces, to music expressly intended for amateur musicians: the *Hungarian Dances, Liebeslieder-Walzer,* and many of his simpler solo songs. He was a talented pianist and an intensely private man, who did not seek to express his musical opinions in print, unlike Liszt and Wagner. His music (and methods of manipulating motives and rhythms) exerted a powerful influence upon later composers—most famously the Second Viennese School.

RELATED TOPICS
See also
THE SYMPHONY
page 76

LUDWIG VAN BEETHOVEN
page 78

CLARA SCHUMANN
page 80

THE PIANO
page 82

3-SECOND BIOGRAPHIES
ROBERT SCHUMANN
1810–56
Highly regarded German Romantic composer; Brahms' most important early champion

JOSEPH JOACHIM
1831–1907
Hungarian virtuoso violinist, chamber musician, and lifelong friend to Brahms; Brahms' Violin Concerto and violin sonatas were composed for Joachim, as were songs for his wife Amalie, a contralto

EXPERT
Katy Hamilton

Brahms grew a beard at age 45, saying "a clean-shaven man is taken for an actor or a priest."

TRIO

pour

Piano, Violon et Violoncelle

par

J. BRAHMS.

Op. 8.

Prix net 10 fr.

THE SCORE

RELATED TOPICS
See also
POLYPHONY
page 24

FRANZ LISZT
page 100

THE CONDUCTOR
page 114

RECORDING
page 136

On one level, it's easy to describe what a musical score is: the representation of a piece of music on a printed page, put there to be read by musicians as actors might read a script. In conventional scores, notes are placed on five-line staves, their position dictating the pitch sounded and the way the note is written indicating its duration. Traditionally, one staff is given for each instrument or part, with piano music notated on two staves and orchestral scores on multiple staves depending upon the forces involved—with individual parts distributed among the players. Music has been written down for centuries in many different cultures, but the score in classical music grew in importance with the growth of printing, becoming essential in the distribution and democratization of music. The score began to become more than a means of dissemination in the nineteenth century with increased interest in music of the past and the publication of editions of works of the Great Composers. The history of the score, therefore, also charts the shift of authority from performer to composer. In Renaissance and Baroque music, much would be left for performers to fill in and improvise. However, scores became increasingly prescriptive throughout the nineteenth century, with ever-more detailed indications of articulation, dynamics, and phrasing.

3-SECOND NOTE

The score—or sheet music—is the name given to music in its written form, on which musicians base their performances.

3-MINUTE REFRAIN

Conventions regarding when musicians should or shouldn't read from scores in performance might seem somewhat arcane. It is normal for chamber and orchestral musicians and piano accompanists to read from sheet music, while usually concerto soloists and piano recitalists perform without scores—emulating a fashion started by the concerts of Liszt in the first half of the nineteenth century—as might conductors with works they know well.

3-SECOND BIOGRAPHY
BREITKOPF & HÄRTEL
founded 1719
Leipzig music publishing house—the oldest in the world

EXPERT
Hugo Shirley

Before recording technology was invented, scores were the only reliable way of distributing music.

IMPRESSIONISM

3-SECOND NOTE
"Impressionism" is usually associated with a school of late nineteenth-century artists, but impressionist ideas have also influenced a wide range of composers.

3-MINUTE REFRAIN
Debussy and Ravel are often associated with Impressionism, but Debussy's music perhaps has more in common with Symbolist poetry's disruption of traditional syntax, while Ravel composed in a number of styles, drawing on older French music, jazz, and Spanish idioms. The central concepts of Impressionism have had a profound influence on many twentieth-century composers. Impressionist harmonies have influenced jazz and film music, while the use of repeated figurations and the concept of timelessness is found in minimalist music.

Impressionist painters were interested in capturing fleeting moments, particularly the changing qualities of light. They made vivid use of color through new techniques that flouted traditional rules. The main composers to be influenced by these ideas were Debussy and Ravel, but the term "impressionism" has also been applied to some later composers, including Bartók and Delius. Debussy's music focuses the listener onto the qualities of sound itself, by exploiting a variety of orchestral colors. Impressionist experiments with the passage of time have parallels in Debussy's languishing harmonies, which invite the listener to enjoy the pleasure of the moment, and in the sense of timelessness created by his use of repeated figures. His music, including *La Mer*, often has a mosaic-like construction. Similar to Monet's *Haystacks*, in which the same subject is repeated from different perspectives, times of day, and seasons, the same melody is repeated with only slight alterations or on different instruments. The colorful harmonies and sonorities of a number of Ravel's descriptive piano pieces, such as *Jeux d'eau*, and the use of sections built from slow-moving harmonies combined with fast-moving "strokes" of sound in his *Daphnis et Chloé* are comparable with the broad sweeps of color and individual brush strokes of Impressionism.

RELATED TOPICS
See also
OLIVIER MESSIAEN
page 144

MINIMALISM &
POST-MINIMALISM
page 146

FILM MUSIC
page 152

3-SECOND BIOGRAPHIES
CLAUDE MONET
1840–1926
French painter; the title of his *Impression, Sunrise* led to the naming of the movement

CLAUDE DEBUSSY
1862–1918
French composer; innovations by him in harmony and timbre influenced later composers

MAURICE RAVEL
1875–1937
French composer whose use of unusual chords and bitonality extended the range of harmony

EXPERT
Joanne Cormac

Debussy's experiments with harmony and timbre produced music of great originality and beauty.

THE RENAISSANCE OF ENGLISH MUSIC

3-SECOND NOTE
Coined by music critic
Joseph Bennett, the
term "English musical
renaissance" suggested a
direct line of descent from
an earlier "golden age" of
English composition: the
sixteenth century.

3-MINUTE REFRAIN
The musical renaissance
was closely allied with
the English folksong
revival movement, led
by Cecil Sharp. (Elgar
distanced himself from this
renaissance partly because
of his antipathy toward
folk music.) Composers in
the early twentieth century
such as Vaughan Williams
cultivated a "pastoral" style
that sought to evoke the
English landscape,
exemplified by the song
cycle *On Wenlock Edge*
and *The Lark Ascending*.
Enduringly popular, this
repertory is sometimes
condescendingly referred
to as "cow-pat music."

In Victorian Britain, music was often regarded as a pursuit for foreigners. But toward the end of the nineteenth century, with national schools of music springing up in Europe, London's musical establishment took active steps to redress the common perception that Britain was a "land without music." The period from the 1870s to the 1890s saw the establishment of important British musical institutions, festivals, and publications, including the Royal College of Music, the Albert Hall, the Proms, and Grove's *Dictionary of Music and Musicians*. Parry and Stanford, both professors at the RCM, led a campaign to cultivate a distinctively "English" musical identity, rejecting the influence of Mendelssohn, so beloved of earlier Victorians. They and their students who rose to prominence in the years before the First World War, including Holst, Vaughan Williams, and Ireland, wrote large numbers of orchestral and chamber works, oratorios, and patriotic songs, a notable example of the latter being Parry's hymn *Jerusalem*. Concerted efforts were made to establish a British school of opera, but although many British operas were written during the late nineteenth and early twentieth centuries, none posed a credible threat to the popularity of the Italian, German, and French repertories.

RELATED TOPICS
See also
MASS SETTINGS
page 34

LIEDER & SONG CYCLES
page 88

PROGRAM MUSIC
page 98

3-SECOND BIOGRAPHIES
(CHARLES) HUBERT PARRY
1848–1918
English composer

CHARLES VILLIERS STANFORD
1852–1924
Dublin-born composer, teacher,
and conductor

EDWARD ELGAR
1857–1934
English composer

RALPH VAUGHAN WILLIAMS
1872–1958
English composer

EXPERT
Alexandra Wilson

Vaughan Williams'
The Lark Ascending
has often been held
up as sounding
distinctively "English."

SERIALISM

A serial composition is typically based upon a single ordering of the 12 notes of the chromatic scale. This 12-note series then forms the basis for an entire composition, being used for both melody and harmony. Schoenberg, the pioneer of the serial method, advocated various manipulations of the series in order to broaden the range of compositional options. For instance, the series could be heard backward, or transposed by different intervals. To many listeners, serial music is as appealing as a prolonged session in the dentist's chair because the perpetual turnover of all 12 notes produces a constant level of acute harmonic dissonance. For Schoenberg and his disciples, however, serial composition offered a way forward for composition following what they perceived as the demise of traditional tonality in the anguished late Romanticism of Wagner and Strauss. Serialism enjoyed a remarkable burst of popularity among younger European composers following the Second World War, when its perceived rationalism chimed with a reaction against pre-war decadence. Figures like Boulez, Stockhausen, and Nono even explored extending the serial principle to rhythm and dynamics. More recently, serialism has become a byword for dry intellectualism in music, and few composers admit to practicing it.

RELATED TOPICS
See also
PATRONAGE
page 70

RICHARD WAGNER
page 104

3-SECOND NOTE
Serialism is a method of musical composition based on a single series of notes. It was first practiced by Schoenberg in the 1920s and gained a wider following after 1945.

3-MINUTE REFRAIN
The fashion for serialism in postwar Europe has been linked to the cultural politics of the Cold War. Idealistic young composers' aversion to the restrictions and conservatism of Stalinist aesthetics here coincided with a US foreign policy that was keen to advertise experimental art as indicative of the freedoms of the West. As a consequence, serialist composers enjoyed considerable patronage from US-funded festivals and residencies in Europe, even in the absence of wide public interest.

3-SECOND BIOGRAPHIES
ARNOLD SCHOENBERG
1874–1951
Austrian composer of the romantic *Verklärte Nacht*, the expressionist monodrama *Erwartung,* and the rational machinations of the serial Variations for Orchestra

ANTON WEBERN
1883–1945
Austrian composer, conductor, and Schoenberg's pupil; he distilled the serial method into chamber works of crystalline brevity and ambiguity

PIERRE BOULEZ
1925–2016
French composer and a leading figure in the development of postwar serialism

EXPERT
Robert Adlington

Boulez's postwar serial music has been likened to a compositional "Zero Hour."

1 2 3 4 5 6 7 8 9 10 11 12

THE TWENTIETH &
TWENTY-FIRST CENTURIES

diegetic Music that can be heard by the characters in a movie because its source, such as a radio, is visible or implied by the action.

extradiegetic Background music used in movies that comes from outside the world of the movie and which the movie characters cannot hear.

leitmotif Term coined by music historian A. W. Ambros in the mid-1860s to describe recurring themes or motifs, usually found in opera, which represent characters, objects, and emotions. Leitmotifs are particularly associated with Wagner's music dramas, which employ a complex web of leitmotifs.

Les Six Parisian artistic group developed from an earlier cultural alliance put together by Erik Satie and called the Nouveaux Jeunes (the New Young Ones). Satie withdrew in 1918, leaving six remaining members (Germaine Tailleferre, Georges Auric, Louis Durey, Arthur Honegger, Darius Milhaud, and Francis Poulenc) whom the critic Henri Collet relaunched in articles instigated by their new backer, Jean Cocteau.

mode An early type of scale developed in order to classify chants to make them easier to learn and remember. Originally, the eight church modes were simply given numbers, but in the ninth century some writers applied the names of Greek scales (such as dorian and mixolydian) to the church modes. Modern Western modes use some of the same Greek names, but otherwise they are quite different from medieval church modes. Modern modes offer an alternative to the traditional major scale as the makeup of intervals is different. They are often found in folk and jazz music, and many composers, such as Debussy and Bartók, have used modes to extend the possibilities of traditional harmony and introduce new and unusual sounds that have an archaic or exotic flavor.

modes of limited transposition Term used by Messiaen to describe collections of notes that can only be transposed (raised or lowered by a certain interval) two or three times, before the same collection of notes is generated. This is due to the symmetry and repetition of intervals within the collection. Accordingly, transposition by certain intervals will actually duplicate the collection of notes. For example, the whole tone scale beginning on C comprises the notes C-D-E-F sharp-G sharp-A sharp.

If we raise (or transpose) all the notes up by a tone, it reads: D-E-F sharp-G sharp-A sharp-C. Therefore, the same collection of notes appears, but in a different order. However, if we do the same thing to the C major scale, the notes change from C-D-E-F-G-A-B to D-E-F sharp-G-A-B-C sharp. Unlike traditional major and minor scales, modes of limited transposition do not create a strong sense of resolution and are, therefore, suited to suggest contemplation and a lack of forward momentum or desire.

musique concrète Term coined by French composer, musicologist, and acoustician Pierre Schaeffer in the 1940s to describe his compositional approach of manipulating and assembling recorded sound. The term encapsulated Schaeffer's aim to work directly with sound rather than with musical notation, not relying on the performer as mediator.

nonretrogradable rhythm A palindromic pattern of rhythmic durations that sounds the same whether played forward or backward. For example, the pattern short-long-short would be palindromic if the short notes are of equal length.

primitivism A term associated particularly with Stravinsky's *The Rite of Spring*. It captures the way Stravinsky's music attempted to depict a crude, uncultured, primitive subject matter, rather than the sophistication of modern life or a beautiful and stylish subject matter.

timbre The quality or character of the sound of a particular instrument or voice or combination of instruments and/or voices.

twelve-tone method Method of composition using all 12 notes of the chromatic scale. The composer places the notes in a fixed order and uses this as the basis for composition, generating harmony and melody from the series. The method is also known as serialism.

RECORDING

RELATED TOPICS
See also
THE CONDUCTOR
page 114

LEONARD BERNSTEIN
page 116

ELECTRONIC MUSIC
page 150

It is difficult to imagine a time before recorded music, or what it was like for earlier generations whose only experience of music was live: in the church, the concert hall, or the home. Today, most music is freely available—in all senses—at the click of a mouse or the swipe of a smartphone's screen. A century ago, with recording only a couple of decades old, acoustic techniques were the norm, which meant that musicians had to crowd around a horn for any chance of being captured on the wax disks. From the 1920s, electric recording meant for the first time full orchestras could be recorded with microphones. Further developments throughout the twentieth century included the postwar switch from 78s, offering some four minutes of music per side, to the LP, providing around half-an-hour per side. The arrival of CDs in the 1980s offered another revolution, designed, it is said, to accommodate Beethoven's 70-minute Ninth Symphony on a single side in clean, crisp, and detailed digital sound. Recorded classical music, and the way it is consumed and distributed, differs in some respects from other music, with recordings offering glimpses of the different ways in which certain core works have been performed over the last century.

3-SECOND NOTE
For over a century classical music has been heard on records and, more recently, CDs and over the Internet, revolutionizing the way we experience an artform that was previously heard only live.

3-MINUTE REFRAIN
At its height, the classical recording industry—like that in popular music—was essential for cementing artists' international reputations, with tenor Enrico Caruso (1873–1921) one of the first to take advantage. In the 1970s and 1980s, meanwhile, German record company Deutsche Grammophon, together with the Berlin Philharmonic Orchestra under Herbert von Karajan created an unbeatable global brand that hasn't been matched since.

3-SECOND BIOGRAPHIES
THOMAS ALVA EDISON
1847–1931
American inventor of the phonograph, the first acoustic recording device, in 1877

STEVE JOBS
1955–2011
American inventor who in 2001, as CEO of Apple, introduced the iPod, the portable device that kickstarted music's digital revolution and threw the record industry into chaos

EXPERT
Hugo Shirley

For a century, recorded music was carried on physical media, while today it is mainly consumed digitally.

IGOR STRAVINSKY

Russian composer Igor Stravinsky (1882–1971) shocked Paris with the 1913 premiere of *The Rite of Spring*, despite the success of his previous ballets, *The Firebird* and *Petrushka*. Outraged listeners heard driving, repetitive rhythms, jarring accents, and complex yet static harmonies. But the now-fabled riots at the *Rite*'s premiere may have had less to do with Stravinsky's sound-world than with the inhuman, angular gestures on stage, or the ballet's grim subject matter: sacrifice of the principal dancer. His music's "primitivism" later attracted criticism for foreshadowing fascist artistic ideals. Almost single-handedly representing a pole within twentieth-century musical aesthetics, Stravinsky's distinctive voice eludes categorization. Partly indebted to his studies with Rimsky-Korsakov, his changing styles divide roughly into "Russian," neoclassicist and serialist periods. He skillfully negotiated and critiqued traditional forms and styles, with tongue-in-cheek symphonies such as Symphony in C, chamber works including his Octet, and operas—*The Rake's Progress*, for example. World politics shaped Stravinsky's career. Exile from Russia in Switzerland and France was followed by emigration to the US after war broke out in Europe again. The image of Stravinsky in the glamor of 1940s Hollywood is difficult to square with his former lives in Russia and inter-war Europe.

3-SECOND NOTE
Primitivist, neoclassicist, proto-fascist: Stravinsky's music has had many labels and its legacy is almost unparalleled, yet the man himself remains enigmatic.

3-MINUTE REFRAIN
Stravinsky was a figure of mythic proportions even during his lifetime. He was the only living composer featured on Walt Disney's 1940 movie *Fantasia*—to underscore warring animated dinosaurs. Stripping away Stravinsky's public persona, however, is challenging. The semi-fictional 2009 movie, *Coco Chanel and Igor Stravinsky*, for instance, projects only who we might like Stravinsky to have been. Although his affair with Chanel probably did take place, sparse documentation leaves much open to speculation.

RELATED TOPICS
See also
THE SYMPHONY
page 76

THE MIGHTY HANDFUL
page 118

SERIALISM
page 130

3-SECOND BIOGRAPHIES
NIKOLAI RIMSKY-KORSAKOV
1844–1908
Russian composer and member of the Mighty Handful

SERGE DIAGHILEV
1872–1929
Russian impresario and founder of the Ballets Russes who commissioned and worked with Stravinsky on his ballets

GABRIELLE "COCO" CHANEL
1883–1971
Iconic French fashion designer who may have had an affair with Stravinsky in 1920

EXPERT
Emily MacGregor

Felia Doubrovska in The Firebird *against original artwork for Vladimir Pleshakov's set design.*

AARON COPLAND

RELATED TOPICS
See also
THE SYMPHONY
page 76

LEONARD BERNSTEIN
page 116

SERIALISM
page 130

IGOR STRAVINSKY
page 138

3-SECOND NOTE
Aaron Copland won over the American public with his "Americana" ballet and orchestral scores, but his modernist, jazz, and Mexican-inspired music reveals the breadth of his eclecticism.

3-MINUTE REFRAIN
Copland seems in some ways an unlikely figure to be so celebrated during his lifetime as a pioneer of American music. He challenged the stereotypical white American masculinity idealized in the Cold War: Not only was he the son of Russian Jewish immigrants and a homosexual, but his communist affiliations during the revolutionary fervor of the early 1930s came under scrutiny in the McCarthy hearings. The willingness of the American public to embrace Copland attests to his music's strength and wide appeal.

New Yorker Aaron Copland's (1900–90) best-known ballet and orchestral scores—*Billy the Kid*, *Rodeo*, and *Appalachian Spring*—carved out a distinctly American sound-world. Yet his stylistic palette went far beyond cowboy Americana, ranging from the jazz-inspired Piano Concerto to the terse modernism of Piano Variations, culminating in his later explorations of 12-tone serialist techniques. His majestic, spine-tingling *Fanfare for the Common Man* has come to symbolize American endeavor and resilience. Over the years it has marked space shuttle landings, the opening of President Barack Obama's inaugural celebration, and the New York 9/11 museum dedication. Besides his own prolific musical output, which further stretched to piano music, symphonies, film scores, and song, Copland fostered the music of other American composers and helped to nurture a direct, uniquely American-sounding style. As a young man, Copland traveled widely, particularly in South America and in Europe, where he received his musical training. *El Salón México*, his first composition to enjoy mainstream acclaim, evoked the Mexican dance halls Copland had frequented with his long-term partner, Victor Kraft. A brief romantic entanglement with Leonard Bernstein led to a lifelong friendship.

3-SECOND BIOGRAPHIES
SERGE KOUSSEVITZKY
1874–1951
Russian conductor of the Boston Symphony Orchestra who set Copland's early career in motion with a commission for the Organ Symphony (1924)

NADIA BOULANGER
1887–1979
French composer, pedagogue, and pianist who taught Copland and many other American composers, including minimalist Philip Glass

EXPERT
Emily MacGregor

Fanfare for the Common Man *welcomed space shuttle* Endeavour *after its final mission.*

GERMAINE TAILLEFERRE

3-SECOND NOTE
Skillfully crafted, and exhibiting the characteristic French virtues of neatness, lucidity, and grace, Tailleferre's best music deserves to be much better known than it is.

3-MINUTE REFRAIN
Tailleferre enjoyed a long and productive career as a composer in a wide range of genres. Among her notable and unusual works for soloist(s) and orchestra were the Concerto for two pianos, wordless chorus, and saxophones (1934), which she rewrote 20 years later as the *Concerto des vaines paroles* for baritone and piano, and a Concerto for wordless soprano (1957), which she revised at the end of her life as the *Concerto de la fidélité*. She became a fluent composer of film scores partly through financial necessity.

Composer Germaine Tailleferre (1892–1983) is best remembered as the sole female member of Les Six, a radical collection of French composers who defined the carefree sophistication of post-First-World-War Paris. Though their artistic aims coincided—albeit briefly—and joint works were occasionally written, the group's ties soon loosened. However, it was the anti-musical-establishment figure of Erik Satie who helped to launch Tailleferre's career. Her own musical predecessors were the eighteenth-century French *clavecinistes* (harpsichordists)—an influence that allowed her musical language to chime with the fashionable neoclassicism of the 1920s. Her large output is uneven, though her Violin Concerto (1936) and the *Cantate du Narcisse* to a text by Paul Valéry (1938) stand out as representative of her best period. Chamber music suited Tailleferre well. Though her operatic career was limited, she produced four little "pocket operas" in 1955, under the overall title *Du style galant au style méchant*. She took naturally to ballet, producing *Le Marchand d'oiseaux* (1923), *Paris-Magie* (1948), *Quadrille* (1949), and *Parisiana* (1953). Though she flirted for a while with serialism, most of Tailleferre's output occupies a harmonic world notable for its ambiguity and subtlety.

RELATED TOPICS
See also
SERIALISM
page 130

IGOR STRAVINSKY
page 138

FILM MUSIC
page 152

3-SECOND BIOGRAPHIES
ERIK SATIE
1866–1925
French composer, whose anti-Romantic music influenced many later twentieth-century artistic movements

PAUL VALÉRY
1871–1945
French poet and intellectual

JEAN COCTEAU
1889–1963
French writer, artist, and filmmaker involved in many artistic enterprises, including Les Six

EXPERT
George Hall

Les Six (left to right): Tailleferre, Francis Poulenc, Arthur Honegger, Darius Milhaud, Georges Auric, and Louis Durey.

OLIVIER MESSIAEN

Born in Avignon, France, Messiaen (1908–92) had emerged as a leading organist and composer before he was imprisoned in a German POW camp after the fall of France in 1940. Messiaen refused to bow to the indignities of camp life and, instead, spent his time composing his 50-minute masterpiece, *Quartet for the End of Time*, with paper and a small pencil smuggled to him by one of the guards. On a rainy day in January 1941, Messiaen himself played a broken-down piano for the premiere with fellow prisoners playing the clarinet, violin, and cello to an audience of 400 prisoners and guards. The eight-movement quartet is inspired by text from the *Book of Revelation*, an important source of spiritual rejuvenation for the profoundly Catholic composer. The composition showcases rhythmic and melodic material characteristic of Messiaen's work. Messiaen was a student of ancient Indian rhythmic practice and palindromic "nonretrogradable" rhythmic passages feature throughout the composition. Messiaen was also a noted ornithologist, and birdsongs he collected appear in the quartet, particularly in the solo clarinet movement, "Abyss of the Birds." Shortly after the premiere of *Quartet for the End of Time*, Messiaen was released from prison. He died in 1992.

3-SECOND NOTE

Messiaen's Catholic faith inspired him to write music of transcendent beauty, even while interned in a German prisoner-of-war camp during the Second World War.

3-MINUTE REFRAIN

Messiaen went on to compose works for forces ranging from solo piano to large orchestra. He was one of the first to experiment with total serialism—applying serial principles to not only pitch but also rhythm, dynamics, and articulation. He became a noted composition teacher at the Paris Conservatoire. He described many of his musical ideas including his approach to symmetrical rhythms and modes (modes of limited transposition) in his influential treatise, *Technique de mon langage musical*.

RELATED TOPICS

See also
SERIALISM
page 130

IGOR STRAVINSKY
page 138

GERMAINE TAILLEFERRE
page 142

3-SECOND BIOGRAPHIES

PIERRE BOULEZ
1925–2016
Renowned French composer and conductor who studied with Messiaen

QUINCY JONES
1933–
American jazz musician who studied with Messiaen at the Paris Conservatoire

GÉRARD GRISEY
1946–98
First French composer of the spectral school, which uses a harmonic language derived from the harmonic series

EXPERT
Elizabeth Kelly

Messiaen's **Quartet for the End of Time** *evokes angels, birds, rainbows, and the Apocalypse.*

MINIMALISM & POST-MINIMALISM

RELATED TOPICS
See also
SERIALISM
page 130

FILM MUSIC
page 152

3-SECOND NOTE
Minimalism is a hugely influential compositional style first developed by American composers in the 1960s and characterized principally by repetition and gradual change.

3-MINUTE REFRAIN
Minimalism has not always had the celebrated status it enjoys today. An early performance of Reich's *Four Organs* at New York's Carnegie Hall triggered loud protests from the audience, and minimalist works have also been booed at contemporary music festivals for committing the solecism of approachability. "Serious" composers such as Elliott Carter and Harrison Birtwistle remained vocal critics of minimalism, but others—notably György Ligeti—found novel ways of incorporating minimalist techniques into more challenging styles.

Minimalism, as the name suggests, originated as a reaction against the pretensions and intellectual complexity of earlier twentieth-century classical music. Early minimalist works focused on simple musical ideas, extended over a long duration via endless repetition or sustained drones. The result was something of an endurance test, challenging limits of perception and patience in a manner influenced by the anarchic concept pieces of John Cage (including his famous "silent" piece, *4'33"*) and contemporary avant-garde art and theater experiments. But in the 1970s the works of Philip Glass and Steve Reich brought minimalism out of the experimental art world and aligned it, instead, with popular and world musics. Classic minimalist pieces like Reich's *Music for Eighteen Musicians* and Glass' *Einstein on the Beach* (both 1976) featured tonal harmonies, funky rhythms, and pop-style vocals. From this point on, minimalism started to attract large audiences and, increasingly, assumed the position of a mainstream style within concert halls and film scores. Minimalist techniques have since proved remarkably adaptable, forming the basis for diverse post-minimalist styles including Louis Andriessen's gritty aggression, Arvo Pärt's "holy minimalism," and the lush symphonic style of John Adams.

3-SECOND BIOGRAPHIES
LA MONTE YOUNG
1935–
American minimalist pioneer. His *Composition 1960 # 7* has two notes and the instruction "to be held for a long time"

STEVE REICH
1936–
American composer of the essential minimalist classic *Music for Eighteen Musicians*; later works engage with the Holocaust, 9/11, and technological threats

PHILIP GLASS
1937–
American composer—possibly the most famous living classical composer—of minimalist works

EXPERT
Robert Adlington

Einstein on the Beach by Philip Glass brought minimalism to a general audience.

1955
Born in Paris

1960
Begins to perform publicly on the cello

1976
Graduates from Harvard

1983
Makes his first recording of Bach's Cello Suites

1997
He is featured on the soundtrack of *Seven Years in Tibet*, with a score by John Williams

1998
Initiates the Silk Road Ensemble

2002
Performs the Sarabande from Bach's Cello Suite No. 5 at the site of the World Trade Center in New York on the first anniversary of 9/11

2006
He is named Peace Ambassador by the UN Secretary-General Kofi Annan

2009
Performs a new work by John Williams at the inauguration of President Barack Obama

2010
Awarded the Presidential Medal of Freedom

2015
Returns in triumph to the BBC Proms with Bach's solo Cello Suites

YO-YO MA

One of the world's leading

cellists, the Chinese-American Yo-Yo Ma has maintained a leading position within the classical world while exploring other musical traditions with consistency and commitment.

Ma was born in Paris in 1955 to Chinese parents, both musicians. Following his move to New York at the age of five, he began to perform on his chosen instrument: At the age of eight he appeared on television conducted by Leonard Bernstein.

Serious studies took place at Juilliard and Harvard. His own development as a musician has included repeated performances and recordings of the great masterpieces of the classical cello repertoire. His interpretation of the six Bach Cello Suites has been recorded twice, and in 2015 he repeated it to great acclaim in a solo BBC Prom at the Royal Albert Hall. He has also commissioned and premiered numerous new pieces, including works by Elliott Carter, Peter Lieberson, and Tan Dun.

In addition, Ma has shown an abiding interest in exploring alternative musical traditions that has led to fruitful collaborations with artists from other genres. The best known of these projects is his Silk Road Ensemble, which connects the music and musicians from all those countries along the ancient route taken by silk merchants traveling from China to the West; between 2001 and 2016 the ensemble has issued six CDs.

Among other projects, there have been explorations of tango, ongoing relationships with jazz pianist Chick Corea and jazz singer and conductor Bobby McFerrin, as well as film composers John Williams and Ennio Morricone, a concentration on the music of Brazil, and a bluegrass album with fiddler/composer Mark O'Connor and double bass player Edgar Meyer. In all, Ma has released some 90 albums which have won him 18 Grammys.

As a classical cellist, Ma maintains a consistent richness and warmth of tone. His playing is technically impeccable, but also full of individual character and touches of personality; each piece that captures his imagination receives a distinctive and memorable response in an approach that combines a larger structural overview with an eye for the smallest detail. Specifically, in his core classical field, his long relationship with the pianist Kathryn Stott has also proved immensely rewarding. He has ranged widely as a soloist from Baroque works to twentieth-century classics, covering virtually the entire standard repertoire of the instrument.

Throughout all this activity, Ma has succeeded in maintaining the respect of his fellow performers as well as the wider public. His commitment to humanitarian projects resulted in his being named a United Nations Peace Ambassador in 2006.

George Hall

ELECTRONIC MUSIC

3-SECOND NOTE
Composers seeking
innovative means of
expression exploited
the empowering electronic
technology of the
twentieth century, radically
influencing many genres of
contemporary music.

3-MINUTE REFRAIN
An unintended result of
the diminishing size and
cost of electronic
instrumentation was its
passage into mainstream
music. The Beatles used a
Moog on *Abbey Road* then
paid tribute to Stockhausen
with *Revolution 9*. Many are
indebted to the work of
the electronic pioneers;
from 1970s progressive
bands such as Pink Floyd
and Kraftwerk, to
electronica artist Aphex
Twin. In 1968, Wendy Carlos
introduced the synthesizer
to the mainstream. Her
Switched On Bach became
the biggest-selling classical
LP of all time.

Throughout the last century the importance of melody and harmony ceded to an exploration of new timbres and unique sounds. This led some experimental composers, such as Varèse and Stockhausen, to compose in purely electronic form. Others, including Hindemith and Messiaen, integrated electronics with traditional instrumentation. Electronics allowed composers to work directly with rhythms, pitches, and timbres in ways beyond any human performer's capabilities. Music could be executed accurately, consistently, and without lengthy rehearsal times. For example, John Cage's *Imaginary Landscape No. 1* (1939) was performed using pure tones played back by vari-speed turntables. In the 1950s composers in Paris developed "musique concrète" by recording and manipulating natural or manmade sounds. Pierre Schaeffer's vision was "to collect sounds and to abstract the musical values they were potentially containing": His *Étude aux chemins de fer* (1948) is made entirely from recordings of steam trains. Composers of Elektronische Musik in Cologne manipulated electronically generated tones. Stockhausen's *Gesang der Jünglinge* (1956) mixed these with sounds from tape. Loudspeakers allowed composers to use spaces in original ways: Varèse wrote *Poème électronique* to fill the futuristic Corbusier-designed Philips Pavilion for the 1958 Brussels World's Fair.

RELATED TOPICS
See also
OLIVIER MESSIAEN
page 144

RECORDING
page 136

3-SECOND BIOGRAPHIES
EDGARD VARÈSE
1883–1965
French composer who famously
asked: "What is music but
organized noises?"

PAUL HINDEMITH
1895–1963
German composer/conductor

PIERRE SCHAEFFER
1910–95
French composer and pioneer
of sampling techniques

KARLHEINZ STOCKHAUSEN
1928–2007
German composer known for
his prolific and groundbreaking
work in electronic music

EXPERT
Simon Paterson

Using similar electronics, new generations of artists are furthering Stockhausen's legacy.

FILM MUSIC

Moving images have long been joined with sound. The earliest silent movies were shown with live accompaniment, usually improvised by a pianist. Gradually, musical accompaniments featured larger ensembles and became more regularized; many studios issued anthologies of ready-made "cues" organized by mood that could be played at appropriate points in the movie. The advent of synchronized sound in the late 1920s represented a considerable leap forward in the potential uses and techniques of film music. Max Steiner's music for *King Kong* (1933) is recognized as a quintessential narrative film score, and is heavily influenced by the styles of nineteenth-century Romanticism. It established the role of leitmotif (musical themes associated with particular characters or situations in the movie), synchronized music and action, and used different styles to suggest mood, character, and location. From the 1960s, the traditional symphonic score was displaced by the use of jazz, electronic sounds, and pop, aimed to appeal to young audiences. However, John Williams' highly successful music, including iconic music for *Jaws* and the *Star Wars* series, became part of a trend back toward traditional symphonic scores. Today, composers such as Hans Zimmer tend to employ a fusion of traditional orchestral and electronic styles, using synthesizers and sampling effects.

3-SECOND NOTE
Many moviegoers pay little attention to a film's score, but film music can have a subliminal and powerful effect, building dramatic tension and manipulating viewers' emotions.

3-MINUTE REFRAIN
Film music can provide continuity, smoothing transitions between camera shots, and plays a vital role in dramatic pacing, building up the anticipation and strengthening the effect of important scenes. It broadly falls into two types: diegetic and extradiegetic. Diegetic music can usually be heard by the characters in the movie because its source, such as a radio, is visible or implied by the action. Extradiegetic or background music comes from outside the world of the movie.

RELATED TOPICS
See also
LEONARD BERNSTEIN
page 116

RECORDING
page 136

AARON COPLAND
page 140

3-SECOND BIOGRAPHIES
CAMILLE SAINT-SAËNS
1835–1921
French composer of the film score to *L'assassinat du duc de Guise* (1908)

ALEX NORTH
1910–91
American composer whose score to A *Streeetcar Named Desire* (1951) was one of the earliest jazz-based film scores

JOHN TOWNER WILLIAMS
1932–
American composer, conductor, and pianist

EXPERT
Joanne Cormac

Early film music usually consisted of a solo piano. Today a vast range of instruments, techniques, and styles are drawn on.

RESOURCES

BOOKS

A Century of Recorded Music: Listening to Musical History
Timothy Day
(Yale University Press, 2000)

After the Golden Age: Romantic Pianism and Modern Performance
Kenneth Hamilton
(Oxford University Press, 2008)

A History of Film Music
Mervyn Cooke
(Cambridge University Press, 2008)

Aspects of Wagner
Bryan Magee
(Oxford University Press, 1988)

Beethoven Hero
Scott Burnham
(Princeton University Press, 2000)

Companion to Medieval and Renaissance Music
Tess Knighton and David Fallows, eds
(Oxford University Press, 1997)

Crescendo of the Virtuoso
Paul Metzner
(University of California Press, 1998)

Electronic and Computer Music
Peter Manning
(Oxford University Press, 2013)

German Lieder in the Nineteenth Century
Rufus Hallmark
(Schirmer, 1996)

Giraffes, Black Dragons, and other Pianos: A Technological History from Cristofori to the Modern Concert Grand
Edwin Good
(Stanford University Press, 2002)

Handel's Dramatic Oratorios and Masques
Winton Dean
(Oxford University Press, 1959)

Igor Stravinsky
Jonathan Cross
(Reaktion, 2015)

Mendelssohn: A Life in Music
R. Larry Todd
(Oxford University Press, 2003)

Messiaen
Peter Hill and Nigel Simone
(Yale University Press, 2005)

*Musicking: The Meanings of Performing
and Listening*
Christopher Small
(Wesleyan University Press, 1998)

*Renaissance Music: Music in Western
Europe, 1500–1600*
Allan Atlas
(Norton, 1998)

The Cambridge Companion to the Symphony
Julian Horton
(Cambridge University Press, 2013)

The Ambient Century
Mark Prendergast
(Bloomsbury, 2003)

*The Cambridge History of Nineteenth-
Century Music*
Jim Samson
(Cambridge University Press, 2002)

*The Rest is Noise: Listening to the
Twentieth Century*
Alex Ross
(Fourth Estate, 2008)

The World of the Oratorio
Kurt Pahlen et al.
(Amadeus Press, 1990)

WEBSITES

BBC Music Magazine
classical-music.com

Samples of numerous classical works
youtube.com/user/ClassicalMusicOnly

Guardian Classical: current articles and live
and CD reviews
theguardian.com/music/classicalmusicandopera

Petrucci Music Library: an online library of public
domain scores
imslp.org

Arnold Schönberg Center Online Music
Manuscripts
schoenberg.at/index.php/en/archiv-2/musik

Steve Reich Clapping Music app
clappingmusicapp.com/

"A Brief Introduction to the Music
of Aaron Copland"
loc.gov/collections/aaron-copland/articles-and-
essays/about-aaron-coplands-works/

NOTES ON CONTRIBUTORS

EDITOR
Joanne Cormac is Leverhulme Research Fellow at the University of Nottingham, working on a project on composer biography. Her research interests include genre, reception, and identity in nineteenth-century music. She has published in leading music journals and her book, *Liszt and the Symphonic Poem*, is forthcoming with Cambridge University Press.

FOREWORD
David Pickard studied Music at Corpus Christi College, Cambridge, before starting his career at the Royal Opera House. After serving as Chief Executive of the Orchestra of the Age of Enlightenment and General Director of Glyndebourne, he took up the role of Director of the BBC Proms in November 2015.

CONTRIBUTORS
Robert Adlington is Professor of Music at the University of Nottingham. He is the author of books on the composers Harrison Birtwistle and Louis Andriessen, and of a study of musical life in 1960s Amsterdam. At Nottingham he lectures on twentieth-century music, musical analysis, and community music programs.

Edward Breen teaches at City Lit College, London, and writes for *Gramophone* magazine. He specializes in the early-music revival of the twentieth century and his PhD—*The Performance Practice of David Munrow and the Early Music Consort of London*—was completed at King's College London under the supervision of Daniel Leech-Wilkinson and Emma Dillon.

Katy Hamilton is a freelance researcher, writer, and presenter on music. She has taught at the Royal College of Music and Middlesex University, and has published on the music of Johannes Brahms and the history of the Edinburgh Festival. She has also made several appearances on BBC Radio 3 as a Brahms specialist.

Kenneth Hamilton is a concert pianist, writer, and broadcaster, Professor of Music at Cardiff University, and author of *After the Golden Age: Romantic Pianism and Modern Performance*.

Monika Hennemann is a lecturer at Cardiff University, musicologist, cultural historian, and linguist with research interests in cultural conflict, transfer, and assimilation in nineteenth-century music, literature, and art of the German- and English-speaking world. She has published on Mendelssohn, Liszt, and "Operatorio" (the theory and practice of dramatic stagings of oratorios).

George Hall writes widely on classical music and opera in particular for a variety of publications, including *The Guardian*, *The Stage*, *Opera Now*, and *BBC Music Magazine*; he is also the UK correspondent of *Opera News* and a member of the board of *Opera*. After taking a degree at the Royal College of Music, he worked as an editor for the Decca Record Co for seven years and in a similar capacity for the BBC for twelve.

Elizabeth Kelly is an American/British composer. Her works have been performed at major venues throughout the United States and Europe including Carnegie Hall in New York, the Huddersfield Contemporary Music Festival in the UK, and the Gaudeamus Festival in the Netherlands. She is an Assistant Professor of Music at the University of Nottingham.

Emily MacGregor is a doctoral candidate in musicology at the University of Oxford, specializing in symphonic music of the early 1930s in France, Germany, and the United States. She has held research fellowships at the Library of Congress in Washington, D.C., and at the Freie Universität in Berlin.

Simon Paterson is Assistant Professor and Director of Music Technology at the University of Nottingham. In demand as a jazz bassist around the East Midlands, since the end of the last millennium he has composed music for TV and film and written and produced records for a wide range of performers.

Owen Rees is Professor of Music at the University of Oxford and a Fellow of The Queen's College, Oxford. His professional work involves both musicology and performance, focusing on the music of early-modern Spain, Portugal, and England. He directs the vocal ensemble Contrapunctus and the Choir of The Queen's College.

Hugo Shirley edited *30-Second Opera* for Ivy Press and is reviews editor at *Gramophone* magazine. Formerly deputy editor of *Opera* and opera critic of *The Spectator*, he continues to work widely as a critic and writer on music for a variety of publications.

Alexandra Wilson is Reader in Musicology at Oxford Brookes University. She has published in many of the leading music journals and is the author of two books: *The Puccini Problem* and *Opera*. She has shared her research with a wider public through numerous broadcasts for BBC Radio 3 and via essays and talks for opera companies including the Royal Opera, English National Opera, Wexford Festival Opera, and Glyndebourne Touring Opera.

INDEX

ACKNOWLEDGMENTS

PICTURE CREDITS
The publisher would like to thank the following for permission to reproduce copyright material:

All images from Shutterstock, Inc. and Clipart Images unless stated.

AKG Images/Erich Lessing: 21.
Alamy/© classicpaintings: 39TC; © Heritage Image Partnership Ltd: 37TC.
Bergen Public Library, Norway: 41BC, 80, 127C.
Getty Images/Annette Lederer/Ullstein Bild: 151TL; Culture Club: 19BC; DEA/A. Dagli Orti Agostini: 75C, 113TC; DeAgostini: 131C; Erich Auerbach: 131C, 141TL; Fine Art Images/Heritage Images: 123CR, 139BC; Frans Schellekens/Redferns: 22; Imagno: 51BC; Isabey/Conde Nast: 143C; Jim Gray/Keystone:153BC; John Kobal Foundation: 153TC; Lipnitzki/Roger Viollet: 143R; Pierre Berger/Ullstein Bild: 145CR; Rob Verhorst/Redferns: 147C; Ron Burton/Keystone: 129TC; Ullstein Bild: 90; Waring Abbott/Michael Ochs Archives: 148.
Herzog August Library: 25TC.
Lebrecht Music & Arts/© Chris Christodoulou: 42.
Library of Congress, Washington, DC: 25C, 63TL, 95BC, 95C, 97TC, 101TC, 101C, 105C, 105R, 116, 119BC, 121CR, 127C, 139TL, 141BL.
NASA: 141BR.
National Gallery of Art, Washington, DC: 11BC, 45BC, 75BC, 99C.

New York Public Library: 37BR, 69C, 95C.
The British Library Board: 19TC, 35B, 35BC, 39C, 41C, 53C, 59B, 69B.
The J. Paul Getty Museum Open Content Program: 11CR, 39C, 45CR.
University of Heidelberg: 29TC.
Wellcome Library, London: 17TL, 21C.
Wikipedia/Marie-Lan Nguyen: 17BC; Sailko: 25BR.
Yale Center for British Art: 51C, 59TC, 61TC, 61BC, 97CL, 129BC.

All reasonable efforts have been made to trace copyright holders and to obtain their permission for the use of copyright material. The publisher apologizes for any errors or omissions in the list above and will gratefully incorporate any corrections in future reprints if notified.